THE PERSONAL WEALTH PLAN

Develop, execute, and control your personal wealth plan to a financial destination of your choosing

DAVID S. UPTON

First Edition

THE PERSONAL WEALTH PLAN

ISBN – 979-8-9851274-1-6 (Paperback)
ISBN – 979-8-9851274-0-9 (Ebook-Kindle)

A very special and heartfelt thank you to Cassandra for leading the effort to transform my private family story about wealth and wealth management into The Personal Wealth Plan that could be shared with all. Her wisdom and perseverance through this endeavor offered clarity to process, structure, and prose that were beyond my training and reach. I truly loved the time spent together working to a shared vision of the message of the story, the tone we hoped to strike, and the reasons we felt this message might be important. Thank you Cassie.

THE PERSONAL WEALTH PLAN

Preface

My Dad passed away on a Saturday morning, March 21, 2009, overlooking the Atlantic Ocean from the beautiful home he and Mom built in York, Maine. He found a lump on his neck in the fall of 2008 and was diagnosed with anaplastic thyroid cancer in late January. Wondering what this has to do with you? If planning for a successful financial future is a priority, I hope you'll allow me this short story to explain.

When he was ill, the family asked my Dad what more he wanted to do while he was living. He told us that he had accomplished everything he set his mind to and traveled everywhere he had ever hoped, a very lucky man. However, he did say the one thing he wished he could have done was to teach his grandchildren how to invest and manage money.

It might not sound like a typical bucket-list item, but investing and managing money had become important to my Dad. He risked everything in the late 1960's to start a company based on a technical insight he developed while working at Raytheon. Dad and a partner started Incoterm, a company that developed the first programmable computer terminals, which were used in airline reservation systems worldwide. The company completed an initial public offering in 1973 and was acquired by Honeywell in 1978. With these transactions, Dad's small portion of the company was worth enough to allow him financial freedom and security.

Before his passing, my Dad asked me to do two things: to call my Mother daily and help her avoid charlatans, and to teach my daughters to invest and manage money for their futures. I've done pretty well with number one but have come to realize I have failed to properly address number two. Sorry Dad. I hope here to more fully comply with your request now that I better understand the importance of discussing wealth and wealth management over long periods of time.

• • •

Introduction

We are going to talk about wealth. We are going to talk about how to accumulate wealth, how to manage wealth, how to spend wealth, how to gift wealth, and how to teach the next generation about wealth.

Wealth is one of those awkward words that can be difficult to discuss. If you have wealth, you might prefer to keep that knowledge to yourself. And if you lack wealth, or a plan for wealth, then the thought of talking about it might make your stomach turn. That feeling will pass, and there is no time like the present, so let's dive in.

You can accumulate wealth by executing a thoughtful plan for your future or, maybe, by being lucky. You might get lucky by winning the lottery, marrying into a wealthy family, or inheriting a fortune. If you're one of these lucky people, you are not excused from the conversation. The world is out to separate you from your wealth. If you want to prevent that from happening, I'd urge you to follow along. I don't believe in luck alone. I believe in taking control of your finances, planning your future, and executing that plan. *With this narrative, I hope to empower you to develop, execute, and control your personal wealth plan to a financial destination of your choosing.*

That word "control" is similar to "wealth" in our culture – nobody really wants to talk about it. Beyond being uncomfortable to discuss, these two words have much in common. You are in **control** of *both* your wealth and your financial future. That is because you, and you alone, are in control of your personal wealth plan.

Executing your personal wealth plan is not complicated and does not take a lot of time. I believe you can plan for your financial future in just a few hours. All told, we need a couple of hours to forge your unique wealth plan, 20 minutes a month to execute the plan, and a handful of extra hours each year to update your personal wealth plan. That's really all it takes.

So, let's discuss wealth, control of your wealth, and your wealth plan, throughout your lifetime and beyond.

• • •

An Offer and an Ask

Before we begin this story about your wealth plan and your control of your financial future, I'd like to offer you a tool that may be helpful to your thinking throughout this process. I'd also like to ask for your feedback about this story so I can better help others.

The offer is simple. This story about your wealth plan will ask you to think about money, lots of money, over long periods of time into the future. This story requires you to think through real-life scenarios to arrive at your personalized wealth plan. You can do this on a yellow pad of paper with a calculator or in an Excel workbook. If a workbook is your preferred means of number crunching, please feel free to use my template to get started. This template will not be perfect for you and will need adjustments along the way as you work with your own information to achieve your financial ambitions, but it will help you to follow the examples posed in this story about your wealth plan. And it might be the simplest way to turn a boring money talk into a ***wow*** money talk that can change your life.

The ask is simple too. When you are done with this story – either for the first time, the second time, or after you've shared it with someone you love – I ask for your feedback. Please help me understand where the thoughts were helpful and meaningful to you and where I may have missed on a topic. Your thoughts and feedback will help me guide the next reader's wealth plan to their intended destination. Feedback of any kind would be greatly appreciated. Thank you.

To request a copy of the template workbook, or to provide feedback, please drop me an email at thepersonalwealthplan@gmail.com. I promise I will not sell your email address and I will not fill your inbox with my own propaganda. And, after working with my editor on this story, I am pretty good at taking criticism – so fire away. I look forward to your thoughts and comments. Again, thank you.

• • •

The Last Chapter

We need to start at the end of your story to see where we are headed. At the end of your story you die. Sorry to start here, but our eventual demise is inevitable. We don't know when our time will come, but on average we are living longer than generations before us, so we need to prepare for the long haul by trusting and following our wealth plan over a long period of time. The "we" I refer to should really be singular because (and I cannot stress this enough) you cannot rely on anyone else to ensure your financial health and well-being. You cannot successfully reach your final chapter by delegating your wealth plan to anyone else, including professional advisors. Financial professionals assume you do not know how to plan and manage your wealth, an assumption that's baked into *their* wealth plan. After our time together, you'll prove the professionals wrong. Throughout this story we'll refer to professional money managers as "your helper," and we'll examine what happens to your wealth plan if you let your helper manage your money. Your helper does not want you to know what I am going to share with you during our time together. Your helper is not your friend, but he or she is going to be envious of your new best friend, your wealth plan.

For most of us, our earned income will stop at some point in life. If we plan for and initiate this change with our own free will, we call it retirement. And if we initiate our retirement, we need to be absolutely sure that the wealth we have accumulated is sufficient to fully fund our retirement and our spending in retirement for a long time.

Enter the 4% rule: If 4% of your accumulated wealth (before-taxes) is enough to cover all of your annual expenses (after-taxes), then you can live forever and never run out of money. If your after-tax requirements exceed 4% of your accumulated wealth, you will run out of money if you live long enough. Please pay careful attention to the 4% rule as you read along.

Stand with me at the end of your story for a moment, and ask, how did I do? If you retired at 60 and died at 90 having consumed only 4% of your wealth (before-tax) to cover your annual expenses (after-tax) then congratulations, you did a great job and we get to talk about gifting your wealth to family or worthy causes. However, if you retired at 60 and died at 90 having consumed all your wealth by 75, 80, or 85, you did a poor job. You did not enjoy your golden years and there is no wealth remaining to gift to family or worthy causes.

So, imagine writing your last chapter, and ask yourself - how honest was I about my plan, about my wealth, and about my real needs in retirement? How true to my plan was I at each chapter in life? How well did I follow the simple rules that apply to me as an individual investor? How and why did I stray, if ever, from the straight and narrow path to wealth? Be honest, please.

• • •

Before the Last Chapter

Let's next go to a place much happier than 'The Last Chapter.' Let's jump to the chapter that begins the moment we choose to retire. Note the emphasis on "choose to retire," versus being forced the workplace later in life and before we are financially ready for retirement.

Your wealth plan should be your friend at this time in life, so you'll be intimately familiar with its key components: assets (home, investment accounts, life insurance), liabilities (mortgage, school loans for the kids, car payments), income (paychecks, dividend income, pension, social security, income from the sale of assets), expenses (both the kind you choose and the kind you don't), and last but not least, tools for turning before-tax assets and income into after-tax money to fund your retirement.

At retirement we will rely on our wealth, along with any pension we earn and whatever public safety net may exist, to pay our bills. Remember, just because your earned income goes to zero at retirement does not mean the bills stop coming, so you need a plan to pay for them. And think about this – when you stop working, you will find you have a lot more time to spend your hard-earned money. You'll need to make sure your wealth plan can keep up.

At the moment of retirement we will likely have a long list of things we want to do and see. We will also be sure to have an honest and detailed plan about our spending each year, and we will aim to have a strong pile of assets large enough that we only need to take 4% each year to make us happy in our retirement. It's all doable, I promise.

• • •

Time in the Market

Warren Buffett writes an annual letter to shareholders of Berkshire Hathaway that is also available to the public (http://www.berkshirehathaway.com/letters/letters.html). I read his letter each year and encourage you to do the same.

In 2018 he told the true story of the first investment he made 77 years ago. He shows us how $1 invested in a no-fee S&P 500 index fund (we will get to this part later if you are not familiar) grew to $5,288 during this 77-year span. Just think, $1,000 invested would have grown to $5,288,000. Four percent of $5,288,000 is $211,520. Could you live on that each year through your retirement? I could. But what if we had invested $1,000 **each year**? How much would we have then? We will do the math shortly, but trust me, it's a lot of money.

Buffett's message here is four-fold: invest as much as you can early in life, pay as close to zero as possible to make and manage your investments, reinvest your dividends, and sit tight for a long time. Regrettably, we cannot go back in time and invest $114.75 as Buffett did in 1942, but we can use these simple and powerful truths to build and execute our wealth plan.

As you listen to friends and colleagues discuss their investments, you will often hear them brag about how they sold this at a market high or bought that at a market low. They are boasting about a concept called "timing the market." Listen carefully and you will find that you never hear friends or colleagues talk about all the times they did *not* time the market correctly.

Our story is not about "timing the market." The story here – as we learn from Buffett– is about "time ***in*** the market".

• • •

The Investment Landscape Has Changed

The landscape for the individual investor has changed drastically during my lifetime. I purchased my first common stock when I was a teenager. With some help from my Dad, who narrowed down the universe of common stocks to just two, I bought common shares in Analog Devices. I remember the deciding reason was that I liked what I read about the president of the company, Ray Strata. I also remember the stock price went up and I made money. Good start.

Like my Dad, individual investors for many years had to make time to research common stocks on their own before taking a leap of faith and buying individual securities. The alternative was to pay a professional stockbroker to create and manage a stock portfolio, enter "your helper." Many investors today still choose to pay for investment advice and guidance. And that's fine for them because we know there are hard-working, knowledgeable financial professionals out there. But do you want to pay a fee to have someone else manage your money? By committing to taking control of your financial future, and with a little time and dedication, you can keep this money for yourself to fund your golden years. Stay with me and I will show you how to beat the pros when it comes to long-term returns on your money.

Years after my first stock purchase, individual investors welcomed another option in the form of the mutual fund industry, which helped them own common stock without having to do the research or pay their helper to do the work for them. In the 1980's and 1990's mutual funds were a way for individual investors to pool their money together with a professional team of money managers and share in a collection of common stocks picked and actively traded by the pros. Mutual funds enjoyed great popularity, in spite of high fees.

In the mid 1970's, John Bogle (founder of Vanguard) invented the first index fund. While mutual funds worked to beat market averages to justify their high fee structure, Bogle's index fund sought to simply match the market with a fee structure as close to zero as possible. The mutual funds are actively managed pools of assets, whereas index funds are passively managed over long periods of time.

Over the last several decades, as information technology has become more pervasive and real-time access to financial data has expanded, investment managers and active fund managers have found it increasingly difficult to beat market averages over time. In an environment of perfect information, the only way for one money manager to win is for another to lose.

The playing field for investment professionals has tilted so far that the likelihood of them beating the market after their fees and trading costs is now only 25 to 40% each year. Think about that – if your helper happens to beat the market (after expenses) this year, how small are the chances they beat the market again next year or over the long term? If your helper's odds of beating the market each year are 30%, then your helper's chance at beating the market two years in a row is 9% (30% times 30%). And your helper's chance at beating the market three years in a row is only eight tenths of 1% (or one time in 125 tries) and those are odds we can't afford to mess with. Fortunately, there is a way you can match the market every year, guaranteed, and without your helper. I don't know about you, but those odds are good enough for me every time.

• • •

Two Examples and a Short Read

You don't have to look far to find volumes of material to support the finding that long-term passive investment in index funds beats actively managed investment portfolios after commissions and fees; I'll share two examples.

The first comes from Warren Buffett's 2017 annual letter to shareholders of Berkshire Hathaway (http://www.berkshirehathaway.com/letters/letters.html). Buffett offers a section entitled "'The Bet' is Over and Has Delivered an Unforeseen Investment Lesson."

Here's a quick summary: Buffett challenged any professional money management firm or team to a 10-year bet, with the victor donating the winnings to a charity of their choosing. Protégé Partners was up for the challenge and employed 200 investment managers working in five separate funds in an attempt to beat Buffett. Meanwhile, Buffett simply made "a virtually cost-free investment in an unmanaged S&P 500 index fund" and did absolutely nothing but reinvest the dividends. Buffett won the bet in a landslide and all the money went to the Girls Club of Omaha, his favorite charity.

The second example comes from my home office. I was handed an investment summary of a not-for-profit corporation that manages a more than $100 million endowment and donates over $3 million to community-based initiatives each year. After reading the summary, I sat down with Excel to see how the fund was performing. It's important to note here that the "helper" in this case had not changed in over 10 years and the data I had was for a 10-year performance history.

In my review I first used the historic data to reproduce the endowment's performance over 10 years of returns after management fees and the annual community initiative funding. I found the helper's annual rate of return was 7.8% each year over 10 years. Now, let's imagine the helper didn't get paid to manage the endowment and the not-for-profit instead passively invested in the S&P 500. The annual return for the S&P 500 over the same 10-year period was 14.7% (an unusual and incredibly high rate of return for this 10-year period), just another example of the passive S&P 500 investment beating the pros almost two to one in the long run.

In this example, had the not-for-profit invested in the passive S&P 500 index fund ***and reinvested dividends***, they could have continued to give away the $3 million (3% compared to the 4% rule mentioned previously) each year and doubled their endowment value to $200 million!

Admittedly, my investment portfolio entering retirement was not $100 million and my annual spending needs are not $3 million, but the point is that if you pay your helper their fee and your helper cannot beat or even match the market, then you will be almost 50% behind the market over the long run, and that can really add up.

A good short read also illustrating this point is "Winning the Loser's Game, Timeless Strategies for Successful Investing" by Charles D. Ellis. A current copy of the book (now in its seventh edition) should remain on your bookshelf or Kindle for you to revisit every few years. I do.

• • •

What Is an Asset?

An asset is something you own (either purchased or gifted) that you intend to sell for a profit at a later time. If you are gifted the family summer home and plan to ensure it stays in the family for future generations, then it may be worth one zillion dollars, but is not an asset in this discussion because you never intend to sell it.

When you invest money to grow your wealth for the future, that investment is an asset. Your stake in the home you own is an asset because you anticipate the value of the home will grow and you expect to sell the home at some time in the future. Your shiny new car is not an asset because it will lose value with time and use. That car is consumption of money, not investment of money in an asset.

• • •

What We Will Buy

We are going to buy exactly what Warren Buffett bought when he won the bet, not because *he* won the bet, but because what he bought will always win the bet for *you*. We are going to buy what he called a "virtually cost-free investment in an unmanaged S&P 500 index fund." You may be familiar with the S&P 500 but if not, let's discuss it further so you can feel comfortable in your understanding of this investment choice.

The S&P 500 is a list maintained by a financial organization called Standard and Poor's of the 500 largest U.S. domiciled, publicly traded companies. Because all the companies listed in the S&P 500 have their corporate headquarters in the United States, they are required to follow U.S. rules and regulations regarding financial reporting and stock trading – which is a good thing for us. It is also important to note that the S&P 500 companies do a lot business outside of the United States. The Thomson Reuters news service estimated that in 2018, roughly 60% of S&P 500 technology-based companies' revenue came from overseas. Standard and Poor's said that foreign sales for S&P 500 companies totaled 43% of revenues in 2017. That means when you buy the S&P 500, you are buying both the U.S. and the world economy in one package – and that is a good thing for us too.

The S&P 500 index fund is a financial instrument that allows us to buy a small slice of all 500 companies at once. The S&P 500 index fund is comprised of common stock ownership in all 500 companies in relation to the market value of each company. That is, if Apple, Amazon, Microsoft, and Alphabet (parent of Google) are valued at 10 zillion dollars and Allergan, FedEx, Kraft Heinz, and Walgreen are valued at one zillion dollars, the S&P 500 will be weighted 10 times more to the first group than the second.

The fact the S&P 500 index fund is unmanaged means the composition of the financial instrument we are going to buy only changes when the Standard and Poor's list of the 500 largest U.S. domiciled companies changes. When a company falls off the list and another takes its place, one stock gets sold and another is purchased, all without changing your piece of the S&P 500 index fund. This limited trading activity results in extremely low expenses within the S&P 500 index fund, yet another good thing.

In support of Buffet's description of the S&P 500 index fund as "virtually cost-free," let's remember that expenses to run the fund are lessened because it only trades when companies exit and enter the list of 500. Also consider that the cost of the trade to buy shares in the index fund (and to reinvest our dividends) has now gone to $0 at most of the places we will be doing our investment business.

Now we know we'll be investing in the S&P 500 index fund, but which ones should we chose? The largest S&P 500 index funds are also the funds with the lowest expense ratios (another good thing). The top three funds we are going to buy are SPY (managed by State Street Bank), IVV (managed by Blackrock under the brand name iShares), and VOO (managed by Vanguard). I own all three, and you will want to own them all too.

• • •

What We Won't Buy

We briefly touched on mutual funds earlier, an asset class that pools together individual holdings of stocks, bonds, or other securities, allowing investors to purchase a position in the collection of individual holdings. When Warren Buffett wanted to buy "a virtually cost-free investment in an unmanaged S&P 500 index fund," he was buying a collection of common stocks, in this case his collection was the largest 500 U.S. domiciled companies. But beware – not all collections of individual holdings are good things for us to consider buying.

If you trust your financial future to someone else, say your helper, you risk not knowing what's in the collections you're buying. This presents two important problems to understand and avoid, one you probably recognize immediately and one you might not see right away.

You probably recognize that if we know nothing about the underlying investments or securities in the collection, we have no idea what our investment is worth. The second issue with this kind of holding is that if you buy it and are not satisfied, your helper is not going to buy it back for the price you paid. Said in financial terms, this collection of assets has little or no liquidity. If you buy this type of holding, you may have nowhere to sell it and the money invested could rapidly head toward zero.

The mortgage-backed securities scandal of 2007-2009 is an example of just how wrong this second issue can go. In this case, the holdings were collections of real estate mortgages from around the U.S. and the world. These mortgage instruments were pooled together (the good credit-worthy mortgages and the properties on their way to bankruptcy) and sold as glimmering assets with no discernable value. Savvy and dishonest "professionals" on Wall Street sold billions of dollars of these bogus securities before the world discovered an important portion of the underlying mortgages was worthless.

The Wall Street banks that created and/or owned these mortgage-backed securities either went bankrupt, were acquired by stronger banks, or were bailed out by the U.S. government and taxpayers. We are not going to allow ourselves to fall victim to any similar scam if, or when, history repeats itself.

If we trust ourselves with our wealth plans, and you should, we avoid any lack of transparency into the underlying value of an investment in a collection of individual holdings that someone else might want to buy for us. Transparency is a key reason why Warren Buffet wanted to buy "a virtually cost-free investment in an unmanaged S&P 500 index fund." Remember, each of the 500 largest U.S. domiciled companies is required to follow U.S. rules and regulations for financial accounting and reporting. Simply put, you and I can read the income statement, balance sheet, and cash flow statement of every company in the S&P 500, that is transparency. If the leaders of these companies misrepresent their financials, they go to jail. I am good with that. For context, please read about Enron (2001) and what happened when the executives in charge misrepresented the company's financial performance.

Transparency becomes an issue when investing in the global economy, perhaps at the suggestion of your helper. You will remember that our 500 largest U.S. domiciled companies do a lot of their business in other countries around the world, 43% in 2017 – and that is good for us. But your helper might decide to bundle a giant group of Chinese growth companies in an index fund called MSCI China A. We are not going to buy these instruments. First, we do not know the financial reporting rules in China. Second, because the communist Chinese government controls the business landscape in that country, we have no say in how and when they change the policies and/or rules that impact the value of the companies in the MSCI China A index fund.

• • •

Another Thing We Won't Buy

You will recall from above that the S&P 500 index fund is a little bit of ownership in the largest 500 U.S. domiciled companies. Bonds, on the other hand, are a little bit of the borrowing done by these large companies, other smaller companies, and the federal, state, and municipal governments. Bonds are commonly issued by the borrower for a fixed amount of time and at a fixed rate of interest. If your helper sells you a $50,000 bond from General Motors at 2.6% for five years, you will be paid $1,300 per year in interest ($50,000 times 2.6%) and you will be repaid your $50,000 at the end of five years.

Your helper might try to sell you on a concept that as you age, you should decrease your exposure to the volatility of the stock market (and to our friend the S&P 500 index) and move increasing percentages of your wealth into bonds. The explanation might be that this move away from the volatile stock market decreases your risk and increases your known income from interest payments on bonds.

When used in science or chemistry, volatility describes how energetic a mixture of ingredients might be. Think of the ingredients in a volcano as very volatile, while pouring a little salt into a glass of water has zero volatility.

The financial world thinks of volatility as a measure of how much any given stock, or portfolio of stocks, moves up and down (or down and up) as compared to the market itself. The market calls this beta. Beta is simple – or we are going to choose to keep it simple. Beta is a number and is equal to one if your portfolio tracks the market perfectly as it moves up and down each minute, each day, each week, and each year. The S&P 500 index is exactly the market, therefore it has a beta equal to one. Portfolios with beta of less than one are intended to go up and down less than the market, while portfolios with beta greater than one go up and down more than the market.

Your helper wants you to have less exposure to market volatility and wants to manage your wealth in a portfolio of stocks that will have a beta lower than one. Your helper tells you that you should let him or her help you avoid scary volatility.

To see how we might feel about beta (and that scary volatility) in our equity holdings, let's have a peak at the "final scorecard" from Warren Buffet's 10-year bet in his 2017 letter to the shareholders. The scorecard can be found at the top of page 12 of his letter. [If you asked for my Excel workbook, open the workbook now and click on the tab at the bottom labeled The Bet.] Look first at the right most column, this is our friend, the S&P 500 index return for each year. We see 10 years and 10 return numbers in the S&P 500 column. The other five columns are the annual returns for each of the five professionally-managed funds Protégé Partners employed during the bet. Ten years times five money managers leaves us with 50 return numbers.

Let's start at the row for 2008. A miserable year for the market, and the year we learned my Dad was sick. The S&P 500 was down 37%. In 2008, because the fund managers built portfolios with beta lower than the market, they all lost less than 37% and beat the S&P 500 index. Good start for the professional managers, but we are in this for the long haul and the next few years tell a different story.

The S&P 500 was up the remaining nine years. Please take a moment and note on the scorecard all the times the fund managers beat the S&P 500 index number. Here is what I found: all five funds beat the S&P 500 in 2008. Other winners were fund C in 2011, fund C in 2014, and funds A, B, and C in 2015. That's 10 wins out of 50 tries. These brilliant professional money managers beat the S&P 500 10 times out of 50 tries? That is a 20% chance of success and an 80% chance of failure.

Before we leave this example, let's look at one other highlight from Buffet's chart in our workbook. If you go to the bottom row labeled "Average Annual Gain" and you average the gains of the five fund managers ((2.0+3.6+6.5+0.3+2.4)/5), you get an average annual gain of about 3%. But if you are going to take out 4% each year to fund your retirement, you will be taking faster than the money managers are gaining (after their commissions and fees). Now look at the Average Annual Gain under the S&P 500 column. If you invest in the S&P 500 index and gain 8.5% each year, your wealth will last forever...as long as you follow the 4% rule.

Now that we know we won't be buying a low beta stock portfolio, let's revisit your helper's claim that bonds will decrease your exposure to the stock market to see if this makes sense for us. And let's keep Buffet's chart from the bet handy.

Let's say you are nearing retirement and have a $3 million investment account filled with S&P 500 index funds. Your helper will advise that half of your wealth should be in bonds to decrease your exposure to market volatility and increase your flow of income from bond interest payments. To remain consistent with previous examples we will use an annual interest rate for the bonds of 2.6% (even though the current long-term U.S. Treasury rate is only 2%). Let's see what happens if you invest half of your $3 million in 10-year bonds paying 2.6% and leave the rest of your money in the S&P 500 index, and because we have the data, the timeframe for this example is over the 10-year period of Buffett's bet.

[If you asked for my Excel workbook, open it now and click on the tab at the bottom labeled Heaps. I think this will help you follow along.]

We start with two equal piles: one $1.5 million stack of 10-year bonds paying 2.6% and one $1.5 million heap of S&P 500 index funds. Ready, go! During the 10-year race, the $1.5 million stack of bonds sends you a taxable interest payment of $39,000 each year, minus the fee paid to your helper (let's say it's only 0.5% since we're dealing only with bonds) so you really get $31,500 each year (after $7,500 of your money goes to your helper to manage half of your money). Your $31,500 each year for 10 years is $315,000 in interest and at the end of the 10th year you find your original $1.5 million back in cash in your account. Nice. $315,000 with no market volatility.

Now let's see what the other $1.5 million heap waiting in our S&P 500 index funds looks like at the end of Buffett's 10-year bet. Refer to your copy of the "final scorecard", specifically the "Average Annual Gain" row. At the end of year one your $1.5 million heap of S&P 500 index funds will have done two things: one, these funds paid you taxable dividends of about 2%, or $30,000 (and you get to keep it all because you didn't pay your helper's fees). Two, your $1.5 million heap of S&P 500 index funds will have grown 8.5% to a heap now worth $1.63 million. To keep this simple and be consistent with the bond example, let's not reinvest the dividends (just this one time) and see how big our dividend pile is compared to the interest pile for the bonds.

We'll see more dividends in year two because we started the year with a larger heap of S&P 500 index funds ($1.63 million compared to our $1.5 million at the beginning of the experiment). And this will continue each year because the average annual gain on your heap of S&P 500 index funds increased by 8.5% each year, allowing you to grow that heap of funds and dividends. Here's where we land at the end of Buffet's 10-year bet: first, your dividend pile is $445,000 – that's $130,000 more than the interest on the bonds your helper wants to sell you. Oh, and your heap of S&P 500 index funds is now worth $3.1 million – that's double what your helper will return when your bonds mature. And you saved $7,500 a year, totaling $75,000 in management fees that would have gone to your helper. I think a little volatility might be alright for us in the long run.

Almost done here, but we need one more example to hammer home the point. Let's say that as you approach retirement, your helper suggests a financial product called target-date funds to decrease your exposure to market volatility. Let's say you put your savings in the target-date fund, tell your helper what year you want to retire, and let them do all the work. No worries, right? Because your helper wants you to be heavy in bonds and light in stocks as you approach retirement, they will constantly adjust your portfolio allocation between stocks and bonds based on how close you are to retirement. If we remember the outcome from the previous bonds versus stocks example, we should be afraid of what happens next...

Let's say your helper started 2019 with half of your $3 million portfolio in bonds and half in stocks because you are close to retirement age. And let's acknowledge that 2019 was an excellent year for the S&P 500. In 2019, SPY (the State Street Bank S&P 500 index fund mentioned earlier) started the year at $252 and finished at $321 for a gain of 27.4% (plus a 2% dividend). If your helper did nothing in your target-date fund you would have had $1.5 million in bonds and $1.9 million in stocks for a total of $3.4 million. But your helper instead insisted on keeping your portfolio at a 50/50 mix of bonds and stocks as you approach retirement. So, he or she spent all year selling stocks (that were still going up) and buying bonds that only pay you 2 or 3%. Thanks for nothing. But let's allow this silly game to play out another year and imagine your helper continues this target-date fund strategy for you through 2020. Where does that leave us compared with where we might be had we simply followed our S&P 500 index fund plan and accepted market volatility even as we approached retirement?

From January 1 until February 19 of 2020 your helper added more bonds to your portfolio to achieve his or her desired 50/50 mix of bonds and stocks, all while continuing to sell your equity shares because our friend SPY moved up to $339 per share. And then all hell broke loose in the form of the coronavirus (COVID-19) pandemic. In the next 33 days the S&P 500 plummeted by 34%. That drastic shift means bonds now make up over 60% of your portfolio, so your helper starts selling bonds and buying equity to get you back to 50/50. Instead of quietly weathering a storm, in the short run, your helper set you up for a turbulent rollercoaster ride, selling equities, then bonds, and finally back to selling equities once the markets calmed and returned to February highs by August.

By year-end 2020, SPY was priced at $374, up another 16.5% for the year plus 2% in dividend payments. From the start of 2019, the SPY fund moved ahead 48% plus the 2% dividend each year. If you had left your $3 million in the old S&P 500 index fund, you would be looking at your investment statement with over $4.5 million in your account. But because your helper wanted to save you from scary market volatility with his or her target-date fund approach, you instead only have just over $3.5 million in your account.

No one loves volatility, but to avoid it seems to mean missing out on markets as they move up over the long term. I am a long-term investor, even in retirement, so I choose to accept volatility in the short term and focus on gains over the long term. More on this as we continue to work your wealth plan.

• • •

How Do We Buy What We Want and What Happens Then?

I suggest you maintain investment accounts with one or more of the top money management firms in the country: think Fidelity, Schwab, TD Ameritrade, or Vanguard. These firms will provide the services you need at the lowest possible cost. Your investment accounts should include an individual (or joint with rights of survivorship, if you are married) investment account, an Individual Retirement Account (IRA or Rollover IRA account), and a Roth IRA account. You should take advantage of services provided by your money management firm to electronically connect your investment accounts to your local bank to deposit a portion of your savings on a recurring basis. You should then execute a buy transaction for one of the S&P 500 index funds: SPY, IVV, or VOO. Let's imagine you open an account and are ready to invest $2,000. If the SPY fund closed trading at $313 per share, you will buy six shares (your $2,000 divided by the share price of $313). It's a simple approach, but please trust me that it will be enough to secure your financial future in the long run, as long as you remain committed to your wealth plan.

As you execute your wealth plan by making deposits to your individual investment account and purchasing more shares of SPY, IVV, or VOO, you'll soon log into your account to find a nifty surprise – free money. And because you have a plan to grow wealth, you'll recognize this as your quarterly dividend payment from SPY, IVV, or VOO, and you know what to do with it. Reinvest every penny back into more shares of SPY, IVV, or VOO.

Markets Go Up and Markets Go Down

We are going to buy "a virtually cost-free investment in an unmanaged S&P 500 index fund," we are going to buy it on a regular schedule, we are going to reinvest our dividends, and we are going to keep it for a long time. We are going to learn not to care about dips in the market in the short term because we are in it for the long haul and over time, we know we'll win.

Let's peek at the value of the S&P 500 since the beginning of 1970 to get a better idea of how the market works over time. This gives us 50 years of perspective, which should be plenty, but feel free to look back another 50 years if you are so inclined and you will see a similar result.

One important distinction before we begin: we have been discussing the SPY, IVV, and VOO S&P 500 index funds in terms of the dollar value of one share. For example, on the last day of December 2019, one share of the SPY fund was valued at $321. The S&P 500 composite index is spoken of in terms of points to measure the combined value of the companies included. So, to measure the market over time we will shift to points and later return to dollars to work on your wealth plan.

On the first day of 1970, the S&P 500 composite index was valued at 90 points. On the last day of 2019, the S&P 500 was valued at 3,235 points, a 50-year gain of 3,490%. Not bad for putting your money in one place and ignoring it for 50 years. Here's another view of this amazing run:

From the beginning of the chart to the end we can see a remarkable ability to grow wealth. However, you must be fully aware of the dismal times that saw the destruction of great wealth along the way. In October 1973, the S&P 500 reached above 111 points and by October 1974 it had dropped to 62 points – a decline of 42% (cause: the Arab oil embargo). The market did not return to its previous high until October 1979 – a five-year recovery period. In September 2000, the S&P 500 reached above 1,520 points and by July 2002 it fell to 797 points – a decline of 48% (cause: the dot com bubble). The market did not return to its previous high until May 2007 – almost a five-year recovery period. And in October 2007, the S&P 500 reached above 1,565 points and by March 2009 it had plummeted to 676 points – a decline of 57% (cause: the mortgage-backed securities scandal). The market did not return to its previous high until March 2013 when it reached 1,569 – a four-year recovery period.

These drops in market value of as much as 50% are horrifying; they will make you sick, cause you to lose sleep, and strain important relationships if you let them. You can get through these difficult periods knowing you have a plan to grow wealth over long periods of time; your wealth plan understands that huge drops in market value are inevitable and recognizes them as buying opportunities. If you have a good wealth plan, and courage, then a 50% drop in market value means you can purchase twice as many shares in SPY, IVV, or VOO. That's a two for one sale anywhere else, so stock up!

Markets go up and markets go down. When you buy during a down market you are reducing the average price you pay for index fund shares and maximizing profit over the long term. The approach you will use over time is called dollar-cost averaging. This approach asks you to invest small amounts every month – whether the market is up or down, just keep accumulating. Your wealth plan dictates that you take the long view over time and come to see these market swings as opportunities. Buckle up, it's going to be a long (and sometimes bumpy) ride.

• • •

Why You Should Own Your Home

For some people, their home will be their biggest and best investment; this will not be the case for us, however, owning your home is a significant and important investment.

Home ownership fits into our wealth plan because paying your mortgage and increasing your equity in this asset is much smarter than paying rent over time. As I've preached to my daughters, you should make a good down payment and borrow money on a fixed rate mortgage to buy your first house. When you sell your house and buy one for more money, you should take all the proceeds of the home sale and use them as a down payment on your next house. If you do not roll all of your gains from the first sale into your second home, you are likely going to pay taxes on your gain (and we want to avoid paying taxes when we can). Another ask while I think of it: keep current on the tax laws, they change often. (We'll take a closer look at tax laws later on.)

You may know by now that I like to use concrete examples to illustrate our investment principles. My Mom and Dad finished building their home overlooking the Atlantic Ocean in York, Maine, in 1989 after buying the land and paying for design and construction. The home sold in 2020 for a nice economic gain after real estate commission and legal fees. The gain on the investment in the home comes out to about 174% over the 30 years they enjoyed the beautiful property. Not bad. Until, that is, you look at what the S&P 500 did in those same 30 years. The S&P 500 was at 353 points in December of 1989 and at 3,243 in December of 2019. That is a gain of 818%. And if you simply reinvested your dividends each quarter for 30 years you would have done way better than just 818% - almost two times better!

Another example: my wife and I built our home in Massachusetts in the spring of 1994. We raised our two beautiful daughters in a wonderful area where neighbors became close friends. We sold that home in late 2020 with a gain on the sale of the asset of about 145% over the 26 years we lived there. Again, not bad, until you compare our return to the market. In the spring of 1994, the S&P 500 was at 450 points and has since gained 620%, and that's without the dividends reinvested each quarter.

Real estate transactions are public records and are readily available on the internet through sites like Zillow or your town or city website. I challenge you to find a dozen residential real estate buy and sell transactions and compare the gain of the homeowner to the S&P 500 gain over the same period of time. You will repeat the above two personal stories almost every time. You should own your home to grow an equity position in this investment and so you don't waste money on rent payments. When you do, and as you continue to work your wealth plan, you'll begin to realize that even your beautiful home will not be your biggest or best investment. Not even close.

• • •

The Importance of Cash

A wise man once said, "It is better to have cash and not need it than to need cash and not have it." Truer words were never spoken; you need cash at every step in life, as it is an integral part of your wealth plan.

When you are working and saving (and investing) for your financial future, you need cash in case the employment that pays your expenses and funds your savings changes in a bad way. If you fall on hard times and have cash to weather the storm, you may disrupt your monthly savings plan, but you will not be forced to disrupt your long-term investment plan to feed your family and pay your bills in the short term.

When you retire, you will need cash so you can choose when accumulated assets are harvested to generate the most possible after-tax income to fund your retirement. When you retire, you will have developed a plan to liquidate assets over time to minimize taxes and maximize the funds you have to spend during this happy time. If you do not have cash on hand in retirement, you may be forced to sell assets either in down markets (below the price points you had planned) or in unfavorable tax positions (producing less after-tax money than you had planned).

When I was a teenager my parents said I should always have what they called "mad money," which was enough money in my pocket so I could extract myself from a bad situation and get home. Their favorite example was if you were on a date that wasn't going well, you would have money to settle your half of the dinner bill and get home safe. Good lesson.

I view "mad money" differently now than my parents did back then. My definition of mad is much worse than a bad dinner date. My definition of mad is that terrorists take down and/or disrupt the power grid of the Northeast or the entire U.S. Think about it, if a terror group succeeds at taking down all electrical power for 60 or 90 days, you will need cash, a lot of it. The ATM machines won't work, your debit and credit cards won't work, the gas pumps won't work, and life will change drastically in an instant. When this happens (and I believe it is only a question of when, not if), you are going to need some serious cash. Another closely held belief of mine is that you should also have a means to protect yourself, your family, your property, and your cash.

Cash is a wonderful thing – we will return to the need for cash as we work your wealth plan toward your retirement goals.

• • •

IRAs and 401(k)s

Individual retirement accounts (IRAs) and 401(k)s are retirement investment tools that should be an important element of your wealth plan. They are categorized as defined contribution plans because you can control what you contribute, you cannot, however, control what comes out later.

As the name implies, the IRA is your individual account and should be held with the same investment management firm we discussed previously (Fidelity, Vanguard, etc.). The standard IRA was created within the federal tax code to allow individuals to deposit before-tax dollars into investment accounts and grow the funds without the burden of taxes. Simply put, the IRA lets you put a certain number of before-tax dollars (ever-changing rules dictate how much you can deposit annually) in your account by April 15 each year. Before-tax, however, doesn't mean this is a free ride – we will have to pay taxes on withdrawals later, but the benefit of growing your money without paying taxes is an essential part of your wealth plan.

A Roth IRA is an important variant of the traditional IRA that allows you to deposit after-tax dollars in an account instead of the before-tax dollars going into your traditional IRA. In the Roth IRA you can invest these after-tax dollars without any further taxes on gains earned the rest of your life. To be able to benefit from the tax-free gains though, you need to commit to incorporating a Roth IRA into your wealth plan, and that means taking the tax hit at the time of your investment. For example, if you make $50,000 a year and pay 22% federal income tax on the next dollar earned, you will have to earn

$2,440 in order to deposit $2,000 in your Roth IRA. It might sound like a lot now, but it will be worth the pain.

The 401(k) is an employer-sponsored retirement plan that allows employees to deposit a percentage of their before-tax salary into a retirement account. This is different than an IRA for two reasons: first, the IRA is a fixed number of dollars each year and the 401(k) is a percent of a salary. Second, the IRA is (usually) a one-time deposit in April and the 401(k) is a weekly (or monthly) deposit and investment throughout the year (think of this as dollar-cost averaging again).

A 401(k) is run by an employer for the benefit of their employees. It's important to note that these plans contain both an upside and a downside. If you have a good personal wealth plan, you may be able to capture the upside and only accept the downside for limited periods of time.

The upside of a 401(k) is that most employer-sponsored plans include a matching provision whereby the employer gives you free money to participate in the plan, typically matching each dollar you deposit up to a limit. For example, if you make $50,000 a year, your employer may match up to 3% of your salary. In that case, if you contribute 3%, your employer will match your $1,500 with $1,500 of their money added to your 401(k) account. If you are fortunate enough to have an employer offering a matching 401(k) plan, ***always*** say yes to the maximum amount of the match! Your wealth plan will thank you for taking the free money. If your salary grows throughout your lifetime at a company, so too will the wealth building in your 401(k) account. Think about contributing 3% of a $500,000 salary instead of $50,000, you end up with $15,000 in free money from your company's match. Hopefully you're able to take advantage of a 401(k) plan, not all companies offer them because they can be difficult to establish due to laws governing participation levels from the earning strata of an employer's organization. That is, these plans require a lot of lower paid employees participate before the highly paid can participate.

Free money is the obvious upside to 401(k)s, but there is a downside. The downside is that "your helper" works for your employer managing the 401(k) program. Your employer's helper will charge you a small fee as a participant in the program to cover the cost of services to run the program, and your employer's helper will limit the investment choices you have to a set of funds that charge fees much higher than SPY, IVV, and VOO and do not provide good market returns.

Here is how we maximize the upside and minimize the downside of 401(k) plans. If our employer offers a 401(k) with a matching provision, we deposit the maximum to get all the free money we can. Then, we take the money out of the 401(k) and "roll it over" into our IRA account, invest it in SPY, IVV, or VOO, reinvest dividends, and, of course, hold it for a long time. You will need to be mindful of 401(k) rules related to when you can take your money out of the plan without forfeiting the free money match, but when the coast is clear, take the money and run.

• • •

Pensions and Social Security

Pension plans and social security are two more potential and important pieces of your wealth plan and should be key considerations when planning for your future. Unlike IRAs and 401(k)s, pensions and social security are defined benefit plans in that they define how much money will be paid to you each month in the future. These defined benefit plans will strengthen your wealth plan by helping you stretch your savings and investments over time.

Unlike 401(k)s, which are gaining in popularity, pension plans have been in existence for a long time. In fact, 401(k)s will most likely replace pension plans in the near future. However, there are still employers who offer both a pension plan and a 401(k) plan - if you're lucky enough to be in that situation.

A pension plan is a retirement account that is sponsored and funded by your employer. If you participate in a pension plan, your future monthly payout benefit is likely based on a formula that includes factors such as your salary, age, and the number of years you have worked at the company. For example, your pension benefit might equal 1% of your average salary for the last five years of employment times your total years of service. Over time, your employer makes contributions on your behalf and promises to provide you with regular, predetermined payouts every month when you retire.

The potential downfall of a pension lies in the fact that your employer funds the pension and likely pays its helper to manage the funds in the pension account and pay out benefits over many years into the future. Each year your employer will note in their financial records the amount they owe the pension fund, but they may not always deposit that full pension liability amount into the pension fund. If your employer does this for long periods of time, the pension fund might not be able to pay your retirement benefits when you begin to expect them.

Social security is like a pension in that it guarantees you a defined monthly payout in your retirement, but instead of your employer managing the payout, it's managed by the federal government. That is a good thing because, unlike your employer, the federal government cannot go out of business. The bad thing is that the payout rules for social security are defined by Congress and are subject to change. This variable leads me to a suggestion you'll see repeated throughout: consider checking your wealth plan before Election Day (more on this later).

While managed by the government, social security is funded by you and your employer each paying 6.2% of every dollar you earn up to an annual earnings limit ($137,700 in 2020). After your earnings reach this annual limit, the social security tax is no longer withheld, and you see an increase in your take home pay until January 1 when the withholding begins again. Congress has traditionally raised this annual limit with increases in the cost of living. Records show the annual limit for the social security tax was $25,900 in 1980, $51,300 in 1990, and $76,200 in 2000.

Your social security benefit in retirement is based on when you entered the system, what your peak earnings and contributions were, and at what age you decide to take the benefit. You can follow your social security benefit by opening an account with the Social Security Administration at www.ssa.gov. Your benefit statement will show your monthly payout benefit if you begin to take the benefit at different ages. For example, your statement might indicate that you get $2,890 per month if you begin to take the benefit at full retirement age (defined as 66 years and eight months for people of my birthdate). However, if you take the benefit at age 62, your monthly check might only be $2,020, and if you wait until age 72 you might receive $3,670 each month.

The tax rules around pensions and social security benefits are complex (and you should do your own homework over time), but the simple logic is that these defined benefits are taxed like ordinary income. So, when we plan your tax on ordinary income a little later on, remember to add this income to your wealth plan at the proper tax rate.

• • •

Credit Cards and Handguns

I have become interested in handguns over the past few years and now have a permit to own guns. I possess the handgun my grandfather carried while walking alone to a train station in Bangor, Maine, to retrieve $1 million in cash that allowed his bank to remain open during the bank holidays of the Great Depression.

But guns are a lot like credit cards. If you use a gun incorrectly, someone is going to get hurt or be killed. If you use credit cards incorrectly, you are going to get hurt or be financially killed.

The single most important rule about using credit cards is that they must be paid off, fully, to a zero-dollar balance, each and every month you use them. If you do not, or cannot, pay them off fully each and every month then you are going to get hurt or be financially killed.

When someone does not, or cannot, pay off their credit card balance, the credit card company charges both interest and service fees. These interest charges and fees on unpaid credit card balances are the same kinds of charges collected by loan sharks (think the mafia). These interest and service charges are in the 18 to 24% range, and higher. These huge fees greatly compound the trouble of the person who cannot pay off the card balance in month one because the balance in month two is 20% higher even before any new charges are added. By the fifth month, the interest charges and fees can double the unpaid credit card balance. These unpaid credit card balances are a death spiral, and your wealth plan does not allow for death spirals.

In an earlier draft of this story, one of my daughters asked that I provide advice for anyone reading this and facing credit card debt –

or maybe you are reading this story and thinking of a loved one who is in this dangerous and deepening hole. I cannot stress enough the importance of climbing out of this hole before you can begin to plan for your financial future and execute your wealth plan. Simple math to convince you here – if you can earn 6% on your investments and are paying 20% on your borrowing, then you are digging the hole deeper and deeper every month. Stop this NOW, acknowledge your situation, and make a plan to pay off your debt. This will be a key component to your wealth plan, which we'll get into later on when we discuss the importance of predetermining your savings and investments by controlling your expenses to fit your earnings – each and every month, forever. In your case, you will be predetermining your plan to pay off the credit card debt.

To budget your way out of this terrible credit card debt hole, I offer you the section of this story called "When You Are Young." It will be hard to do, but you must dig out of this hole one month at a time. With your plan in hand, you should look for a zero-interest way out of this terrible hole. You will look for a zero-interest credit card offer that allows you to transfer your balance and pay no interest for some number of months. If your plan in hand happens to line up with the no interest number of months on the new credit card, then your difficult task just got easier – a lot easier.

If you have found yourself in the depths of credit card despair, don't be embarrassed to acknowledge your situation and ask for help. You'll read in the section "Share the Workload – Share the Knowledge" that sharing your situation and your realistic plan to fix the problem with a loved one may be a crucial advantage to you in climbing out of the hole and moving ahead with your successful wealth plan.

All that being said, credit cards are an important part of our economic life and we will continue to use them. In addition to being a convenient way to purchase everything from groceries to holiday gifts, credit cards also provide a detailed history of spending. Statements can be categorized by expense in Quicken (a personal finance management tool – think electronic checkbook) and easily exported for your annual review of your wealth plan (more on this later).

• • •

What We Have So Far

We have investment accounts at one, or more, of the best investment management firms in the country (Fidelity, Vanguard, etc.) We likely have three accounts with this firm: one for investing our after-tax dollars in our individual (or joint with rights of survivorship) investment account, one for our traditional IRA (or Rollover IRA), and one for our Roth IRA. We know we want to buy the best S&P 500 index funds available (SPY, IVV, VOO) and we want to buy them with $0 transaction fees. We also know we will religiously reinvest our dividends back into these funds each quarter. We may have a pension account and a 401(k) if our employer offers these benefits. And we have a social security account where we can monitor our future defined benefit payments.

We have the knowledge that the stock market will again misbehave and when it inevitably does, it will consume tons of wealth, maybe 50%. We should take some comfort in our understanding that if we follow our wealth plan through long periods of time that these expected reductions represent only a speed bump in our long-term plan to grow wealth.

This point cannot be made firmly enough. While you execute your wealth plan over the long term, the stock markets around the world will provide abysmal returns for extended periods of time. These enormous disruptions will challenge your will and commitment to your wealth plan. Your friends and colleagues will sell in a panic and call you crazy for not running to the exits with them. You will read terrifying stories in the media about the latest financial storm. Your job is to hold your ground, follow your wealth plan, and look ahead

20, 30, 50 years. Your job is to look beyond even the 50% market corrections of the past and remember you are buying SPY, IVV, or VOO at bargain basement prices because your friends and colleagues have panicked. Be strong.

• • •

How Does This Work Over Time?

Time wants to be your friend. Time will greatly aid your wealth plan if you let it, otherwise, time will become your worst enemy.

It's fairly easy to get time on your side: save money (the more time you have, the less you need to save each month or each year), transfer it to your investment accounts, buy SPY, IVV, or VOO, and reinvest your dividends. Let's revisit our old friend, the S&P 500, to illustrate the importance of time to our wealth plan. We can work with these numbers from previous examples:

- 5.3% was the annual growth rate of the S&P 500 that resulted in Warren Buffett's investment of $1 returning $5,288 over 77 years.
- 7.3% was the annual growth rate of the S&P 500 during the 50 years from January 1970 through December 2019.
- 8.5% was the annual growth rate (including reinvested dividends) of the S&P 500 during Warren Buffet's 10-year bet.

If we know the dividend of the S&P 500 is about 2%, then the 8.5% (third example above) that included reinvested dividends from Buffet's bet is about a 6.5% market growth return, which is in the same range as the annual growth rate in the first two examples. Let's assume, for now, that the next 50 years for the S&P 500 are similar to the past 50 years with an average gain of 6% and a dividend payout of 2% each year. Let's use these assumptions to illustrate why time should be your friend.

If we assume a 6% growth on your investment and a 2% dividend each year and say we 1) invest $100 today in your wealth plan, 2) reinvest dividends each quarter, and 3) wait 50 years then, while you were busy doing other things, poof – you have $4,822. Not bad. Now imagine that instead of a single $100 investment, you invested $100 *each month* for 12 months and reinvested the dividends each quarter, now, after 50 years you have $55,383. If you continued to invest $100 each month for 10 years and reinvested your dividends, you would have $399,085 after 50 years. That's why you want time on your side.

[If you asked for my Excel workbook, open the workbook now and click on the tab at the bottom labeled Time. Please take a few minutes to recreate the scenarios in the paragraph above. There are directions on the Time tab to help you along. I urge you to make up your own dollar numbers – the numbers that might fit your life – and start to think about your future.]

If you are going to do the work on your own, open a new Excel workbook, name it "My Wealth Plan," and save it in a prominent location on your desktop (to reference throughout our time together and I hope, as you carry out your wealth plan for the remainder of your life). Label one tab "Time", type the word Growth into cell A1, enter the 6% growth rate of the S&P 500 into cell A2, type the word Dividend into cell A3, and enter the 2% dividend rate into cell A4. In cell B1 type Year, in B2 type Begin, in B3 type Deposit, in B4 type Growth, in B5 type End. Down the column below Year enter the numbers 1 through 50 representing the 50 years in the example above. The "Begin" column below is the beginning balance each year in your account, start with $100. The "Deposit" column is where you are going to enter the other savings you are going to commit to invest over time. In the "Dividend" column, take the "Begin" number and multiply it by the 2% dividend. The "Growth" column is the "Begin" number multiplied by the 6% growth plus the "Dividend" multiplied by half of the 6% growth number (because dividends, on average, are only in your account for half the year). In the "End" column add Begin + Deposit + Dividend + Growth. Now simply let the "Begin" for year two equal the "End" for year one, copy your formulas down the workbook and poof...you have reproduced the math above and hopefully erased any doubt in your mind about the crucial role time must play in your wealth plan.

• • •

Compound Interest

Compound interest is described, by some, as the eighth wonder of the world. Pretty big billing. The Seven Wonders of the World are: The Great Wall of China (China), Christ the Redeemer (Brazil), Machu Picchu (Peru), Chichen Itza (Mexico), The Roman Colosseum (Italy), The Taj Mahal (India), and Petra (Jordan). Quite a list of amazing places you might want to visit in retirement. But why does a financial concept like compound interest often get lumped into a category of the world's most fascinating places? It is important to your wealth plan that you know.

The two-word phrase "compound interest" uses the word "compound" as a verb, so the phrase can be thought of as "to compound your interest" where the verb "compound" means "to put together into a whole, or to combine."

Compound interest is simply a concept whereby you combine your interest with your savings and let them work together as an investment in your future. In our case, when we reinvest our SPY, IVV, and VOO dividends back into more shares of these S&P 500 index funds, we are compounding our dividends and making use of this eighth wonder of the world – compound interest.

If you followed the suggestion above, that you open an Excel workbook and create a worksheet to help you understand how we might invest $100 today and watch as it turns into $4,822 in 50 years, you will recall you added the dividend earned each year to the year-end total and rolled this year-end total into the beginning of the next year. You compounded your dividend into your principal amount and reinvested dividends. You took full advantage of compound interest to turn your $100 investment into $4,822 in 50 years.

To understand the significance of compounding interest (or in our case your dividend) let's remove our dividend reinvestments from the worksheet and see where our $100 investment gets us in 50 years without compounding. [If you asked for my Excel workbook, go back to the Time tab and find the directions labeled "Compound Interest."] You will only have $1,842 after 50 years instead of $4,822 if you did not reinvest your dividends. When we use compound interest in our wealth plan to grow our $100 to $4,822 in 50 years, we have grown our $100 investment by 4,700%. But if our $100 grows without reinvesting dividends, then our $1,842 is only a 1,700% return over time. I guess the eighth wonder of the world – compound interest – is a pretty wonderful thing in our wealth plan, that is, as long as you reinvest your S&P 500 index fund dividends each and every quarter.

• • •

Free Will

Your understanding of the concept of free will is an important component of your wealth plan. Here are three different definitions of free will to consider: first, free will is "the power of acting without the constraint of necessity or fate; the ability to act at one's own discretion." Second, free will is "the ability to choose between different possible courses of action unimpeded." Third, free will is "the ability to choose, think, and act voluntarily." For many philosophers, to believe in free will is to "believe that human beings can be the authors of their own actions and to reject the idea that human actions are determined by external conditions or fate."

I believe that if you understand and exercise the concept of free will, then you can succeed spectacularly with your wealth plan. By exercising our free will, we can plan for saving and investing, choose between saving and consumption, and we can, of our own free will, return to our wealth plan (when prescribed below) to update our plan and hone it through time to achieve a retirement goal and living standard of our choosing. Free will allows us to invest in securities and reinvest our dividends in a manner thought best to achieve our wealth plan goals over long periods of time.

If we surrender our free will and allow someone else to make our important decisions, the result can be emotional and economic disaster. If our decisions between consumption and saving are influenced by outside sources, like friends and neighbors, we will likely lose. If we rush to buy new and shiny investment vehicles because they are hyped by savvy Wall Street insiders, we will likely lose.

Free will is a vital concept in your wealth plan and should be too in your life. God gave us free will, please exercise yours responsibly.

• • •

Hard Choices and One-Way Streets

Let's acknowledge here that the single hardest part of executing your wealth plan is investing the necessary amount each and every month regardless of the real and perceived pressures in your life. I want a bigger house. I want a faster car. I want to go on a cruise. I want a boat. I want to do this because my neighbors did that. I get it. The want to consume more than you earn will never, ever, go away. It is human nature and is fueled by the environment in which we live. My favorite is the Lexus ad at Christmas time. You are a loser if you didn't buy two: one for you and one for your significant other. Those two cars at $100,000 are not in your wealth plan and that $100,000 would have been $4,822,000 in 50 years had you held strong against temptation and societal pressure. Buy the Lexus later in your retirement.

Making the choice to budget your spending so you can commit to your wealth plan is a hard one, but if you are strong and honest, a $100 monthly transfer from your spending account to your investment account becomes a one-way street. I can still hear my Dad's voice in my ear telling me to save my money, invest my money, and never spend my investments. My Dad helped me understand one-way streets.

Another hard choice is what to do with a raise or a bonus. It's in our nature to spend more as our earning power increases. Again, I get it. If you earn $50,000 and get a 3% raise, then after taxes you probably have $100 a month added to your take home pay. If you took this opportunity to double up on the one-way traffic from your spending account to your investment account and invested $200 each month, then for the 10 years of the previous example you would have $809,189 instead of $399,085.

By exercising your free will and trading dinner out a couple of nights a month for an investment in your wealth plan, you are making significant steps to a successful financial future. Now imagine you commit to sending half of every 3% raise over 10 years up the one-way street to your investment account, your friend time will deliver $1,315,149. And if you could continue to invest half of every 3% raise for 50 years, your friend time would deliver $7,161,782. Hopefully you can now begin to see how the concepts of free will and hard choices play a significant role in your wealth plan and shaping your financial future.

[If you asked for my Excel workbook, please head to the tab labeled Streets and follow the directions to reproduce the scenarios in the paragraph above. Again, change the dollar numbers and make them represent your current (or hoped for) situation.]

These are some of the hard choices about spending and saving that your wealth plan requires you make over long periods of time. Your wealth plan needs you to make increasing commitments to savings as your earnings (hopefully) increase each year. These choices will be challenging and are best made by reviewing your written wealth plan on a regular basis. I recommend you do this once a year.

• • •

Predetermined versus Predestined

Your wealth plan requires you to recognize the important difference between two types of events that are going to happen in the future. The first type involves the thing you have no control over. This event is going to occur no matter what you do to try to prevent it. Remember the "Last Chapter"? We are talking about your exit from this earth. You might delay it. You might make it a festive celebration for friends and family. But there is nothing you can do to prevent it from happening. Our eventual demise is inevitable, it is predestined.

The second type of event involves the thing you have total control over. This event will certainly occur because you are going to make it happen. This event is like having scrambled eggs for breakfast on a Wednesday morning. Buy the eggs, crack the eggs in a bowl, get out the frying pan, cook the eggs, transfer them to a plate, and there you have scrambled eggs on a Wednesday morning. Your scrambled eggs are predetermined. You decided on eggs for breakfast and, voila, eggs for breakfast.

Prede(term)ined versus prede(st)ined – almost the same words, just a few different letters, but polar opposites in your wealth plan. People with a predestined wealth plan are hoping (and praying) that the stars align and they win the Powerball lottery, they marry rich, or they die before they run out of money. These people have no real wealth plan at all.

Your wealth plan requires you to predetermine your path to a known and certain financial future. Your wealth plan invites you to predetermine when you will retire and with a specific after-tax spending strategy for your golden years. Your wealth plan asks you to predetermine savings and investing early in your life and asks you to predetermine what you will do with your next raise or bonus before you actually receive that compensation. Your wealth plan asks you to predetermine your choices between consumption and savings so that you are not left hoping there is something left over each month to put away for your future retirement.

Right now, at whatever age you might be, you can predetermine the wealth you will have at any time in your future with a specific 4% goal on a timeline of your choosing thanks to your wealth plan. However, this only works if you exercise your free will and understand the difference between predetermined (you are in charge of your decisions) and predestined (let's hope the stars align and you win the lottery). I know it's hard – like one-way streets, but it is the only honest path to your chosen financial destination. Be strong.

• • •

What Does My Wealth Plan Look Like?

Your wealth plan is an honest view of where you are, where you want to be, and what you are willing and able to do to get there. Its objective is to empower you to plan and control your living standard in your retirement by controlling your savings and investments now. You should create your wealth plan as early in life as possible and you should update and maintain it annually. It is more important that you get started on an honest wealth plan than it is that your initial plan be accurate. Your accuracy will improve with each annual update, you just need to get started and stay on track.

Your wealth plan will include: your current earnings and future earnings potential, your current and future spending (both fixed and discretionary), your current and future savings commitments, your investment commitment (including reinvestment of dividends), your current investment portfolio value, a projection of your portfolio's value into the future, and an honest assessment of your ability to achieve the magic 4% milestone on a timeline acceptable to you and those you love.

Your wealth plan will encompass taxation and the knowledge that only after-tax dollars can be consumed in your retirement. Your wealth plan will include the acknowledgement that inflation is a critical enemy of growing and maintaining wealth over long periods of time.

Your wealth plan will include the real dollars and decisions that are meaningful to your life. The figures in this narrative are meant only to illustrate the functionality of this concept, you need to take this idea of a wealth plan and make it your own. Take from this the shape and sense of savings, investments, taxes, inflation, and spending, and make your wealth plan fit your needs. Use these concepts and illustrations to help shape and realize your personal wealth plan to achieve your goals on a timeline of your choosing.

Your wealth plan will ask you to both look ahead to the future and to reflect on previous events and habits. As we did together at the beginning of this conversation, imagine you are approaching retirement and work backwards. If I plan to consume $10,000 per month forever in my retirement, how much before-tax and after-tax wealth do I need before I initiate my retirement? The magic 4% number would say that we need enough wealth so that if we take just 4% each year before taxes and account for the taxes to be paid, we still produce $120,000 per year (that is your $10,000 per month times 12 months) in after-tax money to spend in your retirement. Since you can only spend after-tax dollars, the tax work in your wealth plan becomes critical to converting before-tax wealth into after-tax spending money for your long and fulfilling retirement.

Your wealth plan will need to become a driving force behind everyday decisions related to spending and saving. Too many people without a wealth plan put off saving and investing for their future until it is much too late. They allow time to become their worst enemy.

Your wealth plan will also come to look familiar to you as you embrace its value and importance over time. Your wealth plan will develop with you as you mature and adjust its make-up and appearance through your lifetime. You will come to look forward to your annual meeting with your wealth plan to ask, “how am I doing,” “what do I do next,” “am I satisfied with my magic 4% timeline,” and “is there something important I am missing”?

• • •

Taxes

Taxes and tax planning are complex topics and can be downright intimidating, but because they both play a necessary role in your wealth plan, we need to work through how taxes function and how they impact your wealth over long periods of time.

When we go to work, regardless of the amount of our wage, our earnings will be taxed. You can see the impact of tax deductions on each paystub you receive from your employer. The paystub has withholdings for federal and state income taxes, social security, state unemployment funds and other withholdings such as a 401(k) savings plan or a health savings account (HSA). The important thing to remember is that you earn your wages before taxes are paid and you (almost always) spend and save your wages after taxes are paid. An understanding of this important distinction between before-tax earnings and after-tax spending is critical to your wealth plan.

For individual taxpayers like you and me, the federal tax system is intended to tax our earnings before we consume them, regardless of whether these earnings are from our physical or mental employment efforts, our investment activities, rent earned on buildings we own, or lottery and casino winnings. The federal tax laws established by Congress are complex (we can argue as to whether they are fair another time) and they change frequently. The current federal income tax code is a progressive tax with increasing rates of taxation that accompany increasing levels of taxable income. This means that someone earning $50,000 a year is currently paying 22 cents on each additional dollar earned while someone earning $500,000 is paying 37 cents on each additional dollar. Despite the complexity of these laws, I've found that simple tax preparation software (from Quicken or H&R Block) can allow most people to prepare their own tax returns each year (emphasis on *each year*, because you will ***always*** pay your taxes).

The congressional and political process responsible for tax laws has resulted in a system with many deductions, exemptions, credits, and loopholes that will likely help to reduce what you must pay. Even with those loopholes and a complicated system, I've concluded there is only one way to avoid paying taxes, but because we don't want to go to prison, we will ensure tax planning fits into our wealth plan. We will always pay our taxes on time because the interest and penalty charges from the tax man are equal to or worse than credit card debt. And we will always work to never pay more tax than we honestly owe.

When individuals file their tax returns on April 15 each year, they fall into one of two categories: those getting a refund and those making payments. You are going to want to be in the second group. I know money coming in always sounds like the better option, but receiving a refund means you loaned your hard-earned money to the federal government for zero interest. If you are writing a check on April 15, then you kept all of your money until the last possible moment. That's what we're going to plan for from now on.

There are two steps to move from category one to category two, but one is a little easier than the other. The easy step is ensuring the amount you have withheld through the end of December is correct and not more than required. You can do this by going to your employer and changing the numbers on your Form W-4, the federal tax withholding form that tells your employer how much to withhold in taxes each paycheck. For example, if you have two children and you enter two children on the Form W-4, you will likely end up in category one and will receive a refund. I suggest you go to the Human Resources department at your employer and ask for help in adjusting your Form W-4 to withhold less money each pay period. They will suggest you make specific changes to line items (maybe related to your dependents) on the Form W-4 or help you calculate the exact amount you want withheld. If your employer's HR department is unwilling to help, either read the directions on the Form W-4 or buy your friend the accounting major a cold beer or two. These changes will move you from category one to category two. On the other hand, you may not have to worry about this piece of the puzzle if you find your taxable dividends in your investment account growing with time because those earnings alone will magically move you to the second category (and I promise, it's where you want to be).

The harder part of moving from group one to group two is taking personal responsibility for having the money ready on April 15 to pay the tax bill. We do this by having a plan to save money each paycheck not only to fund our investments, but to make sure we can pay the tax man in April.

When you start paying the government instead of receiving a refund, there is an important element of the tax code to understand: a provision called the "safe harbor" clause. But before we dive into safe harbor, we need to understand the concept of estimated taxes, which is when the individual taxpayer figures out what will likely be due on April 15 and pays in four installments throughout the year (the 15th day of April, June, September, and January). Each of these estimated tax payment dates is an opportunity to ensure the tax we estimated is still correct. If an element of your tax plan changes, you need to adjust your estimated tax payment accordingly.

The safe harbor clause of the tax laws says that if your deposits with the IRS (the estimated tax payments you might make plus your paycheck withholdings) on January 15 are equal to or greater than your actual tax bill from last year, then even if you owe money on April 15, there is no interest or penalty due. So why does this matter and how can we use it to our advantage? If you are working a regular office-type job and get a refund in April, then when you get an annual raise, your payroll tax deductions will almost always withhold more this year than the tax you paid last year. This means the standard withholding system puts most taxpayers in safe harbor without them even knowing about safe harbor. However, if you are in a profession with the potential to earn large and irregular bonuses and this year's income is much larger than last year, your taxes withheld this year do not have to be any more than last year's taxes. That means you do not have to pay any federal taxes on your expanded earnings until April 15. If you have increasing earnings over time, the safe harbor clause means you can keep your money longer before paying taxes.

The flip side of the safe harbor rule is that if your earnings go down (think a reverse in your large and irregular bonus, or you retire and stop earning a paycheck) then you do not want to rely on safe harbor and pay last year's tax bill if this year's tax bill will be lower. In this case we have to figure out what this year's tax bill will likely be and pay estimated taxes to ensure that the amount on deposit with the IRS is equal to or greater than our actual tax bill next April 15. Exactly how to figure out next year's tax bill will become much easier and clearer as we proceed.

As this is largely a discussion of wealth planning and management, we must also cover the taxes that apply to your investments and when you have to pay these taxes. When you deposit money into a savings account, the bank pays you interest (not much these days) and that interest will be taxed. Similarly, when you invest money in your individual investment account in common stock and the value of the stock increases, you will be taxed on your gain when you sell the stock (called a capital gain because it was earned when you invested your capital). The amount of tax you will pay on your capital gains from the sale of common stock depends on how long you held the investment and how much you earn.

If you buy a common stock for $50 and sell it for $100 less than a year later, your gain of $50 will be taxed as ordinary income. A little earlier we talked about how someone earning $50,000 will pay 22 cents on each additional dollar earned, well these are those additional dollars. If you are the $50,000 earner and you sell this common stock on day 364 after buying it, your taxes will eat up 22% of your $50 capital gain. After taxes your gain is $39. However, if you earn $500,000 and pay 37 cents on each additional dollar, 37% of your $50 capital gain goes to taxes. After taxes your gain is only $31.50.

If instead of selling on day 364 you held the common stock until day 365, you will be taxed on long-term capital gains and those tax rates are lower – much lower. Long-term capital gains are currently taxed at 0, 15, or 20% depending on your income. The $50,000 earner will pay 0% on long-term gains and will keep all $50 of the gain. The 15% long-term gains rate applies to married couples earning between $80,000 and $496,600. Someone earning $500,000 will have to pay 20% but will still have $40 to gain after taxes, which is 30% better than paying short-term capital gains taxes.

Now we know that long-term capital gains taxes are better than short-term capital gains taxes, but is there anything better than long-term capital gains taxes? How about if we didn't have to pay any long-term capital gains taxes for a very long time? You only paid the capital gains taxes in the examples above because you sold your common stock. If you do not sell the investment, you do not pay taxes on your gains (at least in today's tax system).

When you sell your common stock after a year and probably pay 15% in long-term capital gains taxes, the money you have remaining to put back in the market is only $92.50 ($100 from the sale minus the 15% on the $50 gain). To make the point over a longer period of time, let's say you bought a common stock for $100 and held it for a year in which that stock gained 6%. And at the end of the year you sell the common stock for $106, you settle your long-term capital gains tax bill, and invest the remaining funds in a new common stock. If you could repeat this cycle for a long time, say 40 years, you will have turned your $100 into $731, after taxes. After 50 years you will have turned your $100 into $1,202. Wow, even better.

But what if I invested my $100 in the same common stock for 40 or 50 years and never sold, therefore never paying the tax man? If I earned the same 6% as in the example above and never paid taxes, then at year 40 I would have $1,028 (40% ahead the investor who sold after each year) and at year 50 I would have $1,842 (53% more than that now regretful investor). If after 50 years I finally sell at $1,842 and pay my 15% tax on the $1,742 gain, I'm left with $1,581 (32% ahead the investor who sold their stock each year and paid the tax man along the way). The moral of the story is that your 32% ahead can add up over time. Hold your investments for a long time and pay taxes sometime in the way distant future.

We will move on from taxes after one last note on the only thing worse than taxes: double taxes. As you might have guessed, double taxes occur when earnings or wealth are taxed not once, but twice. Two examples are dividends earned on the common stock of a publicly traded company and the estate tax paid at the time of death. There have also been new punitive taxation proposals circulated by one or more recent candidates for president. A topic for another day, but please consult your wealth plan before each and every Election Day.

Double taxation on dividend earnings cannot be avoided. When you own shares of publicly traded companies (and we do because we own SPY, IVV, or VOO and these index funds own shares in the 500 largest U.S. domiciled companies) and these companies pay dividends, these payments will be taxed twice. They are first taxed when the companies file annual corporate tax returns and pay corporate taxes on the profits they earn. The dividends we receive are paid by the corporation in their after-tax dollars. These dividends are taxed a second time when our investment firm (Fidelity, Vanguard) sends us a 1099-DIV at the end of the year with our S&P 500 index fund dividend payments that must be reported on the first page of our annual 1040 tax filing as ordinary income with the IRS. And there you have double taxation (without representation...).

The estate tax (or death tax) is the second example of double taxation but this one, it might be said, is with representation. The estate tax is a tax on wealth at the time of one's death assessed at the federal level and by several states. The 2020 federal estate tax exemption was $11.58 million, meaning that if your wealth exceeded $11.58 million, you would pay 40 cents on each dollar above the exempt amount even though you paid taxes on your earnings and investments while attaining this wealth.

The federal estate tax has some aspect of representation in that Congress has a history of altering both the exemption level and the tax rate as the winds of Washington change. The exemption was first introduced in 1997 at $600,000. The law currently contains a sunset provision that will result in the exemption shrinking dramatically in 2025 unless Congress and the president extend it once again. Current discussion in Washington involves rolling back this exemption for estate taxes to previous levels of either $3 million or $5 million, if not all the way back to zero dollars.

The federal exemption to the estate tax also ties to the notion of gifting wealth during our lifetime, which we will cover a little later on.

An additional death tax is administered in 12 states and varies greatly among them. For example, Maine has a $5.4 million exemption and a 12% rate above that figure. However, in Massachusetts, all wealth above $40,000 is taxed upon death at graduated rates to a maximum rate of 16%. With this in mind, your wealth plan should consider where to reside later in life and embrace gifting of wealth as a tax-planning strategy.

• • •

Inflation

Inflation is an enemy of our wealth plan, a bitter, nasty enemy.

Investopedia says "Inflation is a quantitative measure of the rate at which the average price level of a basket of selected goods and services in an economy increases over a period of time. It is the constant rise in the general level of prices where a unit of currency buys less than it did in prior periods. Often expressed as a percentage, inflation indicates a decrease in the purchasing power of a nation's currency."

That means if you think you need $10,000 a month to pay for the cost of living at the beginning of retirement, you will need more than that each month to consume the same goods and services in the future. The rate of inflation has varied greatly over time; recent figures are in the 1.5 to 2.5% range, however, we don't have to look too far back to find rates in the 4 to 5% range (2007 and 2008) and almost 15% in 1980.

If we use current rates and say inflation runs at just 2% annually, the $10,000 you spend in month one of retirement needs to be $15,000 20 years later to buy the same goods and services. Your wealth plan has to understand inflation and the ravenous impact it can have on consumption over time. And as you work your wealth plan, remember the usual cure for inflation is increased interest rates, which raise the cost of borrowing and decrease corporate profit. Decreased corporate profit reduces stock prices, shrinking your wealth and hurting your magic 4% number.

That is why inflation is an enemy of our wealth plan, a bitter, nasty enemy.

• • •

Last Will and Testament

A will is a legal document that lays out, while you are living, exactly what you want done with your wealth and property when you die. Sorry to revisit this dying thing again, but we cannot overlook the importance of having a will because without one, you have no control over what becomes of your wealth when you pass on. If you die without a will you are deemed to be intestate, meaning the state you live in gets to decide what should be done with your assets. Because you do not want to die intestate, it's vital you make time now to create your will and update it as your life changes.

As you create a will, and if you are doing so to provide for young children in the event the unthinkable happens, you may consider a trust to hold and guard your accumulated wealth (including life insurance proceeds) to fulfill your intended purpose. Your will should be updated to reflect changing priorities in life as your children grow and mature. And as you plan to pass wealth to the next generation(s), you should consider when these recipients might be ready to manage money and ensure they are prepared to do so before substantial assets are within their control – or the control of others in their lives.

Failure to take control of your legacy through a will means an uncertain future for proceeds of your wealth plan, the result of your hard work and saving. If you'd rather this wealth go to loved ones or causes you value, make time to create your will and update it as your life changes.

• • •

Gifting Wealth

You might be reading along and thinking: I don't even have enough money to live well in retirement and now we're talking about giving my money away?! Yes, let's do just that.

Gifting of wealth during your lifetime has a lot in common with the mechanism of leaving wealth in a will through estate planning during your life. Let's start with the rules around gifting and then look at reasons why gifting wealth may or may not make sense during your lifetime.

The first rule to understand is called the annual federal gift tax exclusion, which is the amount of money a gift-giver can give to any one gift-getter in any one year. That amount was $14,000 in 2019 and $15,000 in 2020. This is not the most money anyone can give away, but the most that can be given away to any *one* individual without triggering a filing of the Form 709 Gift Tax Return. If you are the gift-giver and want to make 100 gifts at the annual exclusion level to 100 gift-getters in any one year – no worries, no Form 709 required.

If you gave more than $15,000 in 2020 to a sole gift-getter and filed the Form 709 Gift Tax Return with the IRS, you are allowing the IRS to begin to count your wealth as it relates to your taxable assets at the time of your death. Remember double taxation in the form of the death tax? The IRS starts counting your wealth through your Form 709 filings. The death tax (in 2020) is assessed on wealth above $11.58 million and if you are filing Form 709, your gifting is included in that figure. Here is an example;

Say you did an exemplary job with your wealth plan and accumulated $15 million. First, great job and congratulations. Now you have to worry about that nasty death tax. To avoid the death tax, let's say you gift each of your two children $2 million, leaving $11 million in your estate when you die. It sounds like a good idea in theory, but if you filed the required Form 709 for each of the $2 million gifts, the IRS is now tracking that money and adds $4 million to your estate to assess the death tax. However, if you gave away $4 million by making 267 little gifts of $15,000 each and filed no Form 709 (because you are not required to), then you die under the federal death tax exemption – no death tax. Yes, silly, but true.

As you might have guessed, there are also state-specific estate taxes and guidelines to consider. For personal reasons, I'm going to focus on Massachusetts, but be sure to check your state so you know how this impacts your wealth plan.

Massachusetts has no state-level gift tax and no gift tax return filing requirement. That is, a Massachusetts resident can give away any assets, without limitation, without incurring a gift tax – and these gifts do not count toward the death tax in Massachusetts. So, if you are a Massachusetts resident and your wealth is below the $11.58 million federal exemption and above the Massachusetts exemption (only $40,000), you can gift during your lifetime to fully avoid the death tax at the state level.

Gift giving to charities or other special causes can represent a meaningful use of accumulated wealth if you figure this into your wealth plan over time. You may find religious affiliations, schools and universities, and important community projects to be worthy causes for gifting wealth throughout your lifetime.

The annual gifting of wealth at, or below, the federal annual exclusion level ($15,000 in 2020) is an effective way for families to begin moving money from parents and grandparents to children and grandchildren and can facilitate family discussions about wealth and investing. Annual gifting can serve many purposes, perhaps providing the next generation with a meaningful deposit on a first home, assisting with the costs of higher education, beginning a discussion about investing in S&P 500 index funds, and initiating wealth plans for the next generation. However, I would be remiss if I didn't provide these words of caution: be mindful of who you gift to, how much you gift, and when in their lives the gift-getters receive this wealth. We all want to provide for our families, but can you see a path where children might not benefit from receiving great wealth at a young age? Can you see a scenario where their 4% when they are twenty-something might lead to bad choices and direct them down an unproductive (or even dangerous) path? Or can you see where a twenty-something might disregard the 4% rule and consume wealth with little or no respect for the future. It's something to consider.

• • •

The Basics of Basis

Next on our list to tackle is how we convert your before-tax investment money in our three different investment accounts to after-tax money you can spend in retirement. To do this, we have to understand basis. For some (speaking for my daughters) this is not one of the preferred topics of our discussion, but it's an important one, so please find a comfortable spot to continue reading and we'll have this sorted out shortly.

When you sell an asset, the basis is the part you don't have to pay taxes on because you previously paid taxes on that portion of the asset. Let's revisit your IRA, or 401(k) that you moved into your Rollover IRA (so your employer's helper stopped taking your money to manage your 401(k) for your employer). Because these programs (the IRA and 401(k)) allowed you to save and invest money before you paid any taxes at all, the money will be taxed as you withdraw it to spend in retirement. The basis, the amount you do not pay taxes on, is zero because you never paid taxes on your earnings that funded these accounts. And because the IRA and 401(k) monies were never taxed in your paycheck as ordinary income, these distributions to you in retirement are now taxed as ordinary income. Remember from before, the federal income tax on ordinary income is a progressive tax system where an individual reporting $50,000 of taxable income pays 22 cents on each additional dollar earned and an individual reporting $500,000 pays 37 cents. Planning when you take these dollars out during retirement, and what tax rate you plan to be at, will become extremely important.

After the IRA (or 401(k)) basis, let's look at the basis in your Roth IRA investment account. Remember, the Roth IRA allows you to pay taxes on money on the way into the account in exchange for letting you withdraw it to spend in your retirement without having to pay taxes on the gains you generated over a long period of time. In this case, because you pay taxes on none of the gains, the basis can be thought of as 100%.

Let's look next at how basis works with the $100 we talked about investing for 50 years and (poof...) watching it turn into $4,822. This first $100 is money you earned, paid taxes on, transferred to your individual (or joint with rights of survivorship) investment account, and invested in the S&P 500 index fund. In that example, you already paid taxes on the $100 invested, so that $100 is the beginning of your basis. But your $100 didn't turn into $4,822 in 50 years without you reinvesting dividends back into the S&P 500 index fund. The dividends you reinvested into SPY, IVV, and/or VOO ($1,172 of dividends) are after-tax dividends because you were taxed on these dividends in the year they were paid to you (remember this from double taxation of dividends). Since you already paid taxes on the reinvested dividends, they add to the basis of your $4,822 asset. When you add your first $100 plus the $1,172 in dividends, your basis in the $4,822 to spend in retirement is $1,272. [If you are using my Excel workbook, you can find the roughly $1,172 in dividends by clicking on the tab labeled TimeCalc and adding up the dividends in column D.]

If you subtract your basis of $1,272 from the value of your $4,822 asset, you have a long-term capital gain of $3,650. And when you pay a 15% tax on your long-term capital gain (a tax bill of $547) you have $4,275 in after-tax money to spend in retirement for the $100 investment you made 50 years ago, plus reinvesting your dividends along the way. Not bad.

Basis also has a role to play in the ownership of your home. If you purchased a home for $100,000, we know your basis is $100,000. If you add a two-car garage to the home for $40,000, then your basis increases by that amount to $140,000. It is just like your investment account, when you invest after-tax dollars in your home your basis increases by the amount of the investment. Keep in mind here we are talking about your home as an asset, not a new tractor or shiny car sitting in the garage (remember the section about what is an asset and what is not an asset). For the purpose of basis, we are only concerned with monies invested to increase the value of your home that you will sell for a profit later in life.

To see how this plays out, let's imagine a married couple buying a home together. The basics of basis says that a $100,000 purchase price represents a $50,000 basis for each of the two buyers. Fast-forward a few decades when, after having created many memories in this home, the wife decides to sell it for $200,000 following her husband's passing. Because this woman follows her wealth plan, she must now determine her basis in the home at the time of sale for the purpose of taxes and having money to spend in her retirement.

Enter a concept called "step up." At the time of a person's passing, the basis of their assets steps up to the current market value. In our example, if the market value of the house is $200,000 when the husband passes away, his basis steps up to $100,000, representing the market value of his half. You would then add that $100,000 of his basis to the original $50,000 of the wife's basis and her total basis in the home is now $150,000. If the wife then sold the home for $200,000, she would only have a tax liability on the $50,000 gain and could plan her retirement spending from there. In this case, the husband's basis in the house became tax free when his basis stepped up to market value upon his death. (This is the first of two examples of not having to pay taxes and not going to jail, but you have to die to get this free money. The second way to not pay taxes and not go to jail will be a lot nicer – promise.)

We are going to stay on the basics of basis here, but I first need to point out a tax matter you should remain current on – because by now we know the value of owning your own home. Current federal tax law allows a homeowner to realize capital gains on the sale of their home up to $250,000 for single taxpayers (and $500,000 for married couples) without paying capital gains taxes. This capital gains tax exemption is only available once every two years. But please think carefully before finalizing your sale. If you take a capital gain on your home sale you have to choose what to do with that money. If you consume that capital gain it is gone forever. However, if you reinvest that capital gain into shares of SPY, IVV, or VOO, you might be onto something. Figure it out. This is a fairly new tax rule and will likely change again.

We used a home in the above example, but the concept of "step up" actually applies to **all** assets of an individual at the time they are deceased. Think about this one for a moment and how it could tie into our concepts of investing money, reinvesting dividends, and holding those positions for a long time. Imagine that someone in a generation before you made an investment 50 years ago that grew to significant value at the time of their passing. If this investment was held and not traded or sold, then no taxes were paid during that person's lifetime. At the time of that person's passing, the basis in the investment steps up to market value and the assets move to the heirs (if there is a will) with no taxation on the gain in value over a long period of time.

The basis on assets moving to heirs is the same as a gift you might have received as a birthday or holiday present as a child. If a favorite grandparent gave you a cash gift, it came to you at market value. You did not have to report receiving the gift, you did not have to pay taxes on the gift (because your grandparent did), and you were free to spend or invest the money with that invested amount representing the new basis in your investment. You were probably pretty good on the basics of basis before we started this conversation and didn't even know it.

• • •

The Process of Developing and Managing Your Wealth Plan

Your wealth plan will evolve and mature as you remain committed with your time, your mind, your financial resources, and your realistic goals for the future. The process of maintaining this wealth plan will involve a weekly component, a monthly component, and an annual component.

The weekly component of your wealth plan is simple and will take just five minutes. I suggest you sit down sometime between Friday at 4 p.m. ET (when the stock market closes) and 9:30 a.m. ET on Monday (when the stock market opens) and record the price of SPY, IVV, and/or VOO in the Excel workbook you use to track your wealth plan. [If you asked for my workbook, open it now and click on tab at the bottom labeled Weekly. You might find some historic price data for SPY, IVV, and VOO to get you started.] If you are doing this on your own, then open a new worksheet and label it "Weekly." Enter Friday's date in the left-most column, use the index fund symbols for the column headers next to the date column, and enter the prices for SPY, IVV, and VOO after the trading week is complete. Next week, enter Friday's closing prices on the row below. If you miss this time window you can always go to www.finance.yahoo.com and look it up later.

I think of this weekly component of your wealth plan as a reminder – in two ways. First, it is your weekly reminder that you have a wealth plan and you are working to set and achieve a financial goal of your choosing. Second, it is a reminder of the hard choices you have made to set a predetermined savings and investing amount for each week and each month. I think that as you enter the prices of SPY, IVV, and

VOO each week you might be reminded of either, when you cheated on your plan during the past week – or where you held strong – either is a good and healthy reminder to help you stay on track.

The monthly component of your wealth plan is also simple and will take just 15 minutes. This is where you revisit the commitment you made to yourself as to how much you are investing each month. You are also going to check to see if SPY, IVV, and/or VOO paid your quarterly dividends. It will take a few minutes to log into your account, make your monthly purchase, and reinvest any dividends. I do this on the first weekend of the month because SPY, IVV, and/or VOO pay most dividends later in the month.

The annual component of your wealth plan will take a little more time, and that time commitment will increase as you move through life. You'll need to pick a time of the year for an annual review of your wealth plan, and a long look in the mirror will help too. I always use October to update my wealth plan and I don't worry about when in October (first week, middle, last week, all good). I just make sure that I am done before Halloween. I picked October for two reasons. First, October is nowhere near the year-end holidays. I did not want to be working on hard choices and one-way streets at that time of year. Make your hard choices in October and then don't overspend during the holidays. Second, October is always just ahead of the election cycle in November. Updating your wealth plan before an election offers reflection on choosing among the candidates and other opportunities we will cover in the pages ahead.

• • •

A Summary and a Question Before We Proceed: Think You Can Beat the S&P 500?

To this point, we have focused on the tools necessary to develop your wealth plan during each stage of your adult life. The sections that follow are focused on the actions you should think about taking during each of these stages and how to predetermine your standard of living and your after-tax spending when you choose to retire.

Throughout the previous sections we have stressed investing, and reinvesting dividends, in S&P 500 index funds – namely SPY, IVV, and VOO. We have carefully noted that these regular and predetermined investments in "a virtually cost-free investment in an unmanaged S&P 500 index fund" will develop great wealth to fund your retirement over time to a goal of your choosing. We have shown that this is a better approach than actively-managed investment portfolios, after fees and trading costs, because today's investment professionals cannot beat the market over time.

By now you may be thinking two things. First, that buying the S&P 500 index every month is boring, boring, boring. I get it. Second, that you could be smarter than the S&P 500 index and should try your hand at buying other assets that will beat the market over time. I get that too. So, let's have that discussion before we move onto thinking about your wealth plan at each stage of your life.

To have this discussion let's set a simple ground rule or two. First, if you must stray from the boring S&P 500 index funds, then let's agree that you will only put a small portion of your investment funds at risk.

Let's agree you will move no more than 5% of your total holdings into some other investment to see how smart you are. Second, let's agree that you will keep track of how your new investment performs compared to the S&P 500 (including reinvested dividends). If the evidence shows you are not as smart as the S&P 500, then you will admit you were wrong, you will sell the other asset, and you will return those funds to SPY, IVV, and VOO. Good? Here are a few thoughts on how to step away, just slightly, from our friend the S&P 500 index.

The S&P 500 is a group of diverse companies that operate in a broad set of industries and is organized by sectors representing specific industry types. These sectors include communication services, consumer discretionary, consumer staple, energy, financials, health care, industrials, information technology, materials, real estate, and utilities.

Insight into sectors of the S&P 500 allows a case to be made that if you invested in a sector you thought would perform better than the overall market, you might do a bit better than the S&P 500. Let's see how that theory plays out, starting in technology.

I can offer three technology-focused index funds that might represent the technology sector. They are QQQ (a NASDAQ related index fund managed by Invesco), FSPTX (Select Technology index fund managed by Fidelity), and IYW (U.S. Technologies index fund managed by iShares). Right off the bat these funds have two disadvantages to the S&P 500. First, they pay almost no dividends, so they have to make up for that with pure price growth to keep up with the full return of the S&P 500. Second, their expense ratios are much higher than the S&P 500 so, again, pure price growth has to compete with our reliable friend, the S&P 500. The expense ratio of QQQ is seven times higher than IVV and FSPTX is 24 times higher. Pick your new poison carefully.

Armed with this knowledge, let's say you still want to explore one of these funds. You first must figure out how to make this investment without paying taxes on any long-term capital gains you have earned on your S&P 500 holdings. You have two options. First, you could redirect your monthly savings allotted for your S&P 500 investment to this new sector. Second, you could sell S&P 500 holdings in your

IRA, 401(k), or Roth IRA account because you don't pay taxes on those funds when you realize a capital gain. The choice to do this in your IRA, 401(k), or Roth IRA account is the winner every time.

If you bought QQQ at the beginning of 2019 at $153 per share, you would have earned 40% through the end of 2019 while the S&P 500 index gained only 30%. [And if you requested my Excel workbook you might find these historic QQQ prices next to the SPY, IVV, and VOO columns in the Weekly tab.] You would have beat the market by 10%. Not bad. And if you had the wisdom to hold this QQQ position through 2020, your shares would have grown to $314 per share, or you doubled your investment in 24 months while the S&P 500 advanced 50%. Now, if you had invested in QQQ at the beginning of 2015 at $101 per share and held this position through 2020, you would have tripled your investment in QQQ while the S&P 500 was up by 85%. Not bad again.

If you invested 5% of your holdings in QQQ in 2015 and it has moved up 210% while the S&P 500 has moved up 85%, you now have more than 5% of your holdings in QQQ. Your QQQ holding is now 8% of your total portfolio and your S&P 500 index funds are only 92%. Remember here our first rule: because we agreed you will allocate no more than 5% of your portfolio to this experimental holding, it's time to rebalance your positions. To return to a 95 to 5 balance between S&P 500 and QQQ you will sell some QQQ and buy some S&P 500. This rebalancing should occur in your IRA, 401(k), or Roth IRA account so you avoid creating long-term capital gains taxes. By doing this you are letting your gains compound over time.

The second example of stepping away from our friend the S&P 500 index relates to working the annual component of your wealth plan in October (because it is a long way from the year-end holidays and just before election season). On the first Tuesday in November 2016, the country elected a new president promising (among other things) to strip away decades of regulation and red tape for U.S. businesses large and small. If one followed the news, including the financial news, one might think that smaller U.S. businesses could benefit from deregulation and red tape taken off the profit and loss statements and that their stock value might rise faster than the larger companies represented by the S&P 500.

The IWM (Russell 2000 index fund managed by iShares) index fund is a grouping of the 3,000 largest U.S. domiciled corporations minus the 1,000 largest, leaving you with an index fund of 2,000 U.S. domiciled corporations representing smaller companies. If you invested 5% of your holdings in IWM after the election and held the position until the end of August 2018, you would have beaten the S&P 500 by 10%. However, if you held your IWM position until August 2019, you would have found yourself 10% behind the S&P 500. This dramatic turnaround is due to trade tariffs introduced by the president at the end of August 2018. [Again, if you requested my Excel workbook you might find these historic IWM prices next to the SPY, IVV, VOO, and QQQ columns in the Weekly tab.]

Remember here our second rule about straying from S&P 500 index funds: if it turns out you are not smarter than the S&P 500, you will liquidate your new position and return to the S&P 500. If you did not heed this advice after the trade tariff threats of August 2018, your IWM investment would still be more than 10% behind the S&P 500 at the end of 2020 with a dividend of only 1% instead of the 2% paid by SPY, IVV, and VOO.

[If you asked for my Excel workbook, open it now and click on tab at the bottom labeled Weekly. If you want to try and beat the S&P 500, then you might want to add a few columns to track the funds you want to put that 5% of your wealth into. Recording these prices each week – along with the SPY, IVV, and VOO prices – will help you keep track of your attempt to beat the S&P 500.]

In closing, there are alternatives to help you beat the S&P 500. But with them comes work, guessing, fees, and probably some angst. Maybe the boring S&P 500 isn't so bad after all.

• • •

When You Are Young

The weekly and monthly components of your wealth plan will not change over time, but the annual component will change significantly.

The first review or two in your earlier years is about getting comfortable with the tools you need over time to create, improve, and maintain your wealth plan to a financial destination of your choosing and within your control (this is where your free will comes into play). When it comes to the annual review, your accuracy will improve over time, so don't stress about getting everything perfect the first time or two. Let's just start a new habit that will play a large role in making your financial dreams a reality.

Open the Excel workbook you saved as "My Wealth Plan" on your desktop. Now open a new worksheet that you might want to label "Income and Expenses." [If you asked for my workbook, go back to the Young tab to get started. Here you will see your actual earning and spending at the top and your plan to save and invest money in the coming months directly below in the section "Your Wealth Plan Moving Ahead."] On this worksheet you are going to record your income and expenses for each of the past 12 months. The expenses are a summary, not all the details. We want one row that says groceries, not an item for each time you bought food during the month. I use Quicken (a popular finance management tool) for our personal finances and checkbook so my annual look at spending is to simply export the year by spending category. If you do this annual component of your wealth plan in October (because it is not too close to the year-end holidays and just before elections), then your monthly columns will run from October to September. That becomes your planning year.

If at this moment you're racking your brain trying to find a way to summarize a year's worth of groceries and Amazon deliveries, no worries, I have two easy solutions for you. The first is to recreate your financial transactions. Find your pay stubs, bank statements, credit card and/or debit card statements, or your Venmo account details, and focus on just the last month. From these accounts, figure out what your take home pay was and where all the money went.

Next, do the same thing for the month prior and put those expenses in a column next to expenses for the first month. That is, month two groceries are next to month one groceries, same for gasoline, rent or mortgage, clothing, and those Starbucks lattes. And when you do the groceries line, please use a separate line for eating out or Uber Eats/GrubHub meal delivery. Just work your way back for, maybe six months, and then go back two paragraphs and try again. If you cannot rebuild your financial steps with this method, starting today, keep track of your income and expenses and return to two paragraphs above when you have some information to think about.

Now that you can clearly see your monthly expenses for the past 12 months (or however many months you've worked through for now) take some time to look carefully, and probably alone, at where you spent your money in the last year. Are you comfortable with where it went or do you want to make some changes in the 12 months ahead? Just answer the questions honestly for yourself. It is ok to get up and walk away to think this through. I never do my annual update in one sitting, it is usually done over a span of days (but it is always done before Halloween). A hint for you here. If this first look at your spending in the past 12 months has a big bucket called cash (or maybe debit card), then maybe you can work during the next 12 months to track differences between gasoline (probably necessary to get to work) and $7 Starbucks lattes (maybe that's a lot of expensive coffee) or between groceries for cooking at home and meals out or Uber Eats/GrubHub meal delivery. The point here is that you have to be able to see it to be able to think about it.

At this point you've gained undeniable visibility into your income and expenses. With this knowledge you are going to make a monthly commitment to predetermined savings and then plan your income and expenses to fit that predetermined savings plan. Hard choices, right? Balancing this predetermined savings with your income and expenses may take more than one try, and that's okay. Make this predetermined savings commitment as big as you can but not so big that you will fail to save this amount for 12 months in a row. We care more that you do this for 12 perfect months in a row than we care about the actual amount each month. We are building a behavior over time. Remember that once you send your predetermined savings up the one-way street to predetermined investing, that you still need to pay bills and zero out your credit card each month. Document this commitment to predetermined savings in your Excel file and have this amount automatically transferred up the one-way street to your investment account either once a week (divide your monthly savings commitment by four) or once a month, but before you complete the monthly component of your wealth plan by logging into your investment account to invest money and reinvest dividends.

During your annual review you'll also want to think about your plans for any raise or bonus you might receive within the next year. How much of your after-tax increase can you commit to send up the one-way street to your investment account? That's right – we are going to plan now for money you hope to get in the future. If someone earning $50,000 annually gets a 3% raise, they'll see about $100 in additional monthly income after taxes. If you had an extra $100 per month, can you commit to split that evenly between investment and consumption? It will make a difference if you can. Document your decision so you'll know what to do when you get that well-deserved bump in your paycheck. And don't forget to come back to this step next year and ask, how did I do?

There is one last thing I want you to do during your first annual review. I want you to go back to your Excel workbook – hopefully the one you requested and I sent to you. [Let's use the tab labeled Young – Next Step to see what your wealth plan tells you about your commitment to savings at this point in your life. You are going to find directions in blue type after a bullet point and will be directed to enter your real data into the yellow cells. First, enter the real balance of your investment accounts (all three of them – your individual investment account, your IRA account, and your Roth IRA account) into the yellow cell B12 next to Current Balance. Second, enter your real annual salary in cell G1 (or hourly rate times the hours you work each year – 2,080 hours is 40 hours per week times 52 weeks). Third, enter your current guess (and a guess is okay because you are young and the plan will get more accurate with time) at a raise percentage each year in the future in cell G2. This is a guess at how much your pay will increase each year while you are working.

Now let's be bold for a moment. Click on cell G3 and enter the percentage of your future raises (after taxes) that you have committed to save and invest in your future. Just to start – I suggest you enter 50% in cell G3. Look at the numbers in column F in rows 13 through 21. I hope you are looking at some big numbers. The number in cell F17 is what your investment balance will be if you commit to this savings and investment plan for 30 years. And cell F19 is for 40 years and F21 shows you the 50 year number. This may be the first time you are looking at what you can save and earn if you follow your wealth plan for the rest of your life. Congrats. Good work.

Now let's reflect on a few topics that you will learn more about as you move through this story and through your life. Two items to consider here are inflation and taxes. The value of your future investments after 50 years might look like a very nice number. But now you need a quick look at what will happen over time with inflation and taxes you'll need to pay before you can use that money to buy groceries in your retirement. Click on cell H10 and on the down arrow and click on 2%. The "Likely Value" at 50 years represents the impact inflation will have on your wealth over time. Now click on cell J10, on the down arrow, and click on 15% for taxes. The value in cell J21 is your likely monthly withdrawal from your investment accounts in 50 years after accounting for inflation and following the 4% rule. Please play with this worksheet to understand your commitment to saving and investing while you are young.]

If you are young and are following the suggestions in this section – chief among them to make a commitment to invest some amount each month, reinvest your dividends each quarter, and invest a committed portion of your coming raise and/or bonus – then you may decide to skip the next three sections, as they are really not intended for you. Please feel free to continue reading so you can begin to understand the long road ahead, but don't worry too much if this discussion seems complex at first glance. It will become clear and obvious over time. On the other hand, if you are not as young as you might like to be, please read on.

• • •

When You are Not as Young as You Might Like to Be

There is a middle stage in your life, probably when you're not as young as you might like to be and before you are ready to retire, when you and your wealth plan need to see, formulate, and understand how and when you might *choose* to retire. Remember, this ideally is when ***we*** make the decision to stop working (on our terms, not someone else's) with the knowledge and confidence that our wealth plan can finance our chosen lifestyle for a long time.

At this time in your life, as you contemplate when you might retire, the annual component of your wealth plan needs to focus on understanding what your annual spending will be in retirement and where these monies will come from. The reason you looked at income and expenses each year when you were young was to begin thinking about spending in the future.

As you ponder your future expenses, you should consider which costs you can reduce or eliminate, and which expenses will continue forever. For example, you will choose to pay off your mortgage to decrease a large monthly expense, but you cannot stop the property tax bill from coming. You will have purchased life insurance when you were young and starting a family, but you will choose to stop paying for it when your children are grown and your wealth plan can provide for your spouse if you are gone. You will have found that health insurance is a huge monthly bill (when you pay for it individually), but that cost decreases considerably when you are eligible for Medicare. Carefully review your monthly and annual expenses and think through which of these may change over time.

As you begin to understand what your future expenses may be in retirement, you will also start to realize how much money you will need to fully fund your retirement by combining your ongoing monthly income (remember defined benefit sources like pension and social security, as well as dividend income from your investment accounts) and applying the 4% rule to your projected investments. For example, $10,000 a month to spend in retirement equates to $120,000 a year after taxes are paid. But if you expect pension and/or social security to provide $2,500 a month after taxes, you only need $7,500 a month after-taxes from your investment accounts in the form of dividends and liquidation of some small part of your S&P 500 holdings. It's time now to think through that process, the dollars, and where they will come from.

The after-tax part – now that's the harder part. But remember, this is a process. Right now your goal is to think through how your savings and investments can fund your spending in retirement – it's linking the past to the future. Your accuracy will improve over time and your understanding of hard choices and one-way streets will sharpen. Promise.

During this long middle part of your life, when you are not as young as you might like to be, you will want to have money in three different investment types with three different tax consequences. We covered these earlier when we discussed taxes, IRAs and 401(k)s, and The Basics of Basis. To recap, your Roth IRA deposits were taxed on the way into your account, so all of your accumulated wealth in the Roth IRA is after-tax money. Next, we have your IRA and 401(k). You will recall that these deposits were never taxed on the way into your accounts, so they must be taxed as ordinary income when you withdraw these funds to spend in retirement. And last, we have your individual (or joint with rights of survivorship) investment account, which allowed you to invest your after-tax dollars and after-tax dividends to form the basis of your total investment value to determine the long-term capital gains taxes you will owe later in life. At this point in your life, when you're not as young as you might like to be, but before you leap into retirement, you need a tax plan as part of your wealth plan to ensure you have sufficient after-tax funds to spend in retirement.

With the goal of developing this tax plan, we can now apply our knowledge of these investment accounts, and our defined benefit programs, to convert these holdings (actual or planned) into after-tax dollars to help you think correctly about spending after-tax dollars in retirement.

First, let's review the federal income tax brackets for 2020. Remember, tax rates are set by the political process in Washington so this will change during your lifetime and will need to be updated as part of your annual wealth plan review.

[If you received my Excel workbook, click on the tab labeled Tax Chart and focus on the tax rates and income levels in cells A1 through G8. If you opted not to ask for my workbook, look up the current Federal income tax brackets and follow along.]

As we look at these tax rates for different levels of income, remember that we are going to determine how much income we want to generate in any future year of our retirement by carefully deciding what assets to liquidate based on the tax implications and our anticipated cash needs. What I see in the table above are three simple bands of tax rates. The smallest band contains the 10% and 12% rates, which really don't allow for much income. The largest band contains the 32%, 35%, and 37% rates, which look like more taxable income than I probably need to spend each year in my retirement. So, I set my tax plan around the middle bands of the 22% and 24% tax rates.

But please note that the 24% tax band is only for the dollars earned between $171,051 and $326,600 for married couples ($85,526 and $163,300 for single tax filers). The lower rates apply for all of the taxable income before $171,051, so your average tax rate is less than the band you identify yourself within. It's vital that you do the arithmetic through each tax-rate band and figure the actual rate you should plan with. For our work together we will continue to plan with the 22% tax rate. [But if you asked for my Excel workbook, click on the Tax Chart tab, enter your expected income in cell J1 and find your real planning rate in cell H10 if you are married or cell D10 if you are filing taxes as a single person.]

Once you've identified your tax rate you can next apply it to your IRA/401(k) investments in either your real savings today or your plan for savings in the future. Let's say we have $1 million in our IRA/401(k) (or our plan is to have $1 million in our IRA/401(k) when we retire). We have to plan for the taxes when these funds are withdrawn as ordinary income after we retire. When we pay 22% in taxes on this $1 million in our IRA/401(k) we are left with $780,000 to spend in retirement.

We will also pay taxes on assets funding our retirement from other sources, like the monthly benefits we expect from our defined benefit programs (social security and pensions) and dividends earned on our S&P 500 index fund holdings in our taxable individual (or joint with rights of survivorship) investment account. These payments from social security, pensions, and dividends in our taxable investment account will also be taxed as ordinary income.

Suppose now that in addition to the $1 million above in our IRA/401(k) account we also were fortunate enough to have accumulated $1 million in our Roth IRA and another $1 million in our individual (or joint with rights of survivorship) investment account. We know that the $1 million in the IRA/401(k) account will get us $780,000 to spend in retirement, but do the other two $1 million investments allow us to retire if we want to spend $10,000 per month forever?

We know (from above) that the money invested in the Roth IRA, which has now grown to $1 million (or will in your plan over time), was all invested in after-tax dollars with a promise that future withdrawals be tax free. Therefore, the $1 million in the Roth IRA is also $1 million to spend in your retirement. That's good news. But what about the $1 million in your individual investment account where you also invested after-tax dollars?

Your individual (or joint with rights of survivorship, if you are married) investment account at Fidelity, Vanguard, or Schwab is money invested after taxes along with dividends invested after taxes. These after-tax investment amounts represent your basis in your investments. When you log into your investment account you will find a current dollar figure showing your cost basis in your investments in SPY, IVV, and/or VOO. Simply take the total value of your investment account and subtract the cost basis to estimate the long-term capital gain you will pay in taxes on over time. Now multiply that gain by the long-term capital gains tax rate of 15%. But remember, the good people in Washington mess with this tax rate from time to time, so stay informed and update your wealth plan in October before you vote. I strongly recommend that you vote with your wealth plan in mind (but you probably already knew that).

Back to our example: if you have $1 million in your individual (or joint with rights of survivorship) investment account and your cost basis is $400,000, you have to account for long-term capital gains taxes before you can spend the after-tax money in retirement. That's $600,000 in long-term capital gains times 15%, resulting in $90,000 in taxes to pay over time and leaving this account with $910,000 in after-tax funds to spend in retirement.

Let's use the above example to see where we end up after taxes if we have $1 million in each of the Roth IRA, traditional IRA, and individual investment accounts. If the goal we set earlier in life was to apply the 4% rule to $3 million in before-tax funds and take $10,000 a month, forever, to fund our retirement, how did we do? In the Roth IRA we plan to pay no taxes. That's a clean $1 million. In the traditional IRA we have to pay a lot of taxes, so that $1 million is only worth $780,000 in after-tax planning. And in our individual investment account, $1 million turns into $910,000 after we pay the tax man his long-term capital gains tax over long periods of time. Altogether, our $3 million in before-tax investments (or planned investments) is only good for about $2,690,000 in after-tax wealth. That gives us $8,960 a month if you are living by the 4% rule. Can you afford to cut $1,040 from your plan to spend $10,000 each month? Would your significant other be happy if you told them you slashed your retirement spending plan by $1,040 a month or $12,480 a year? Or, do we have more saving and investing to do so we can afford to pay the tax man before spending after-tax dollars in retirement?

Let's remember that our $2,690,000 in after-tax wealth does not yet take into account the interest and dividends we receive or the defined benefit payments we expect in the future. Let's see where we wind up with those two key components of our wealth plan in mind.

Since we are not as young as we might like to be, let's continue to plan to reinvest all of our dividends into additional shares of SPY, IVV, and VOO. Let's not consider any dividend payments as a source of income to pay for expenses in our retirement. On the other hand, future monthly payments from our social security with the federal government and our pension plan with our employer (if you have one) *can* be factored into our future spending after we account for taxes.

Remember from the section above that social security payments and pension benefits (almost always) will represent ordinary income and will be taxed at the same 22% rate that we used for our IRA/401(k) withdrawals. If our monthly social security payment is known to be $2,500 per month before taxes and we pay 22% in ordinary income tax, then we are left with $1,950 per month in after-tax money to spend in our retirement.

If we add this $1,950 after-tax social security money to the $8,960 after-tax money from our investment accounts, then we might have $10,910 each month to spend in our retirement. And if our goal is to spend $10,000, then this extra $910 per month might begin to represent a necessary cushion for inflation – the bitter enemy of our retirement planning.

[If you have my Excel workbook please head to the tab labeled Not as Young. If you don't have my workbook you will have to work through this recursive exercise on your own. The "Before Tax Investment Accounts and Balances" section reflects the example above: $1 million in each of your three accounts. The after-tax work is right below in that same tab in the "After Tax Investment Positions" section. You will see the 15% long-term capital gains tax on the individual (or joint) account takes the after-tax position to $910,000, the ordinary income tax at 22% takes the IRA account to $780,000, and the full value of the Roth IRA flows through to after-tax money.]

[The left side under "Sources of Income" shows you how to think about the money you will need each month to buy groceries in your long retirement. Monthly social security income would be known from your account with the Social Security Administration. Your pension amount would be known through your employer, if you quality for a pension. Your dividend income would be the 2% dividend paid on your individual (or joint) account. These amounts of ordinary income would then be taxed at the rate you expect, and the rate used here is 22% we discussed above. Add to this amount the 4%

of your after-tax assets in cell K13 and you have a view of the amount you might be able to spend each month in retirement.]

If at this stage in your life, you begin to combine your investment planning and defined benefit planning to achieve your monthly spending goal in retirement, you begin to take more concrete steps to achieving the financial goals you identify and refine within your wealth plan. Remember, this will not be perfect right away, or even after a few tries, and that's ok. If you let time be your friend, you can afford to adjust your spending and saving for investments while you still have a ways to go before you want to retire. This is just one step in being honest with ourselves and honest with our wealth plan.

[I would urge you to return to the Young tab of the Excel workbook and focus on the right most column labeled Retire. Think through each expense category you identified and work to a retirement number for each line. If you pay off your mortgage, then that line goes to zero but the property tax continues to go up. Cash in your life insurance and eliminate that expense. Sign up for Medicare at age 65 (you hope...) and your healthcare costs decrease. Use this tab to work your expense planning with the income planning on the Not as Young tab.]

[Your job is to work the bottom section of the Not as Young tab to begin to see the wealth plan that fits your reality and your hopes for the future. As earlier, you are going to find directions in blue type after a bullet point and you will be directed to enter your real data into the yellow cells. This tab uses the information from the work you did on the Young – Next Step tab to estimate the future value of your individual (or joint) account, so you will want to keep this updated. Back in the Not as Young tab, you will enter your current age and the age at which you hope to retire in cells D19 and D20. Beginning at row 26, you will see separate input sections for your IRA, Roth IRA, and 401(k) accounts. If you do not have one or more of these, just enter zeros in the yellow cells. For the accounts you do have, enter the information in the yellow cells.]

[Beginning at row 39, you will see the same summary of investments and monthly money as was shown for the example above. But this time you're seeing these numbers as components of your personal wealth plan – your view of your possible financial future. On the right side, at cell K40, you see the expected value of your individual (or joint) investment account (from the Young – Next Step data you entered) projected out until the year you said you wanted to retire. You will need to scroll down to cell G58 and enter your guess/estimate for the basis of your investment account. I offer you the range of 30-40% and I loaded the cell with 40% as a starting place for you. The dollars in cells K41 and K42 represent your IRA, 401(k), and Roth IRA balances at your retirement goal. The amount in K50 is the after-tax value, that when multiplied by the 4% rule and divided by 12 months tells you what you can count on from your investments to buy groceries in your retirement.]

[The left side of the Not as Young tab is the same as above. However, this again is intended for your real data – not to illustrate one more example. Please enter your expected monthly social security benefit in cell C40 and any monthly pension benefit in cell C41. The dividend number is driven by your investment account to the right and the tax burden is the result of your work on the Tax Chart tab. The Monthly Amount in cell C50 might be the monthly income you can begin to think about having to buy groceries in your retirement. This is your tool to think through and to work your wealth plan. Please use it often and use it wisely to the destination of your choosing.]

Please listen carefully here. Like others who are working their wealth plan to a specific target over time, I love to see the prices of SPY, IVV, and VOO go up, and up, and up. However, even if your total investment number finally hits $3 million (or whatever your goal is) you must still determine your after-tax dollars when you sit down with your wealth plan each year. So, yes, cheer the before-tax market prices of SPY, IVV, and VOO, but live in the reality of your after-tax spending in retirement.

For those of you I'm speaking to in this section, if you have followed my suggestions – chief among them to start bridging the gap between today's spending and the spending you anticipate in retirement, learning to view your current and planned investments in after-tax dollars to spend in retirement, and developing an honest view of your retirement wealth goals through the 4% rule –you may decide to skip the next two sections, as they are really not intended for you. You are of course welcome to read them to understand the next pieces of the long road ahead, but don't worry if they seem complex at first glance.

They will become clear and obvious over time, just as I hope this section has become clear to you with time. For those approaching the edge of retirement, I encourage you to read on.

• • •

When You Approach the Edge, but Before You Leap

We each may approach the decision to retire from different and unique directions with some trepidation and maybe with unknowns and uncertainties. But *you* will approach the decision to retire with a firm and honest understanding of your wealth plan and what you have accumulated to this point in life. You will have a clear understanding of the after-tax dollars available to you to spend in your retirement. You will also know what defined benefit payments (pension and social security) you can expect and when they will become available to you.

Let's start with the simplest situation as you approach the edge but before you leap, even though this scenario may not be your situation or mine. In this situation you are approaching your 67th birthday and your social security benefit can begin immediately at $2,890 per month (let's use my earlier example of full retirement age being 66 years plus eight months). You have no pension, but have been diligently working your wealth plan for a long time. You want to spend $10,000 per month in your retirement and have accumulated $2.7 million in before-tax investments that you figure are about $2.4 million in after-tax funds to buy groceries in retirement.

Our after-tax investments of $2.4 million multiplied by our 4% rule provides us with $96,000 to spend each year or $8,000 to spend a month. When we pay the 22% ordinary income tax on our $2,890 monthly social security payment, we are left with $2,250 to add to our $8,000 and we have $10,250 in monthly spending money. Your responsibility at this point is to go back and check the tax consequence of your defined benefit social security payment. It will depend on how you got to your after-tax 4% number from your investment accounts, and it will be important, so don't forget to go back and do this tax homework.

Let's assume that your $10,000 per month spending plan includes $1,200 a month to pay the mortgage on your home (and we are going to own our home). As you approach the edge and before you leap, you need to look at your mortgage value, your monthly mortgage payment, and the 4% rule. Now let's answer the simple question "should I pay off my mortgage now or keep making monthly mortgage payments in retirement?" If your mortgage value (the amount you still owe the bank) is $150,000, that represents money in your investment accounts that belongs to the bank. If you pay off your mortgage, then your investment accounts go down by the amount that belongs to the bank (with tax implications of selling your financial assets to repay the bank). What should you do?

Well, if your mortgage value is $150,000 and we apply the 4% rule to that mortgage value, then the $150,000 in your investment portfolio (that amount that really belongs to the bank) is only providing you with $6,000 per year or $500 per month. So, if the mortgage value (in your investment accounts) is providing only $500 per month and your payment is $1,200, you should pay off your mortgage before you leap. Now finish the math about where this paid off mortgage leaves you. With expenses at $10,000 per month (mortgage payment still in), your social security, and 4% on your $2.7 million, you had $10,250 to spend. But if you pay off the mortgage, your $2.7 million goes down to $2.55 million and your 4% gets you $90,000 per year or $7,500 per month. That investment withdrawal plus your after-tax $2,250 from social security provides you with $9,750 per month. By paying off your mortgage, your $10,000 monthly expense is cut by $1,200 to $8,800 and you are ahead by $950 per month (think about our nasty enemy named inflation, having this $950 cushion will really help...).

Now that we feel comfortable with the situation above, let's complicate the matter to more closely parallel real views you might have of retirement and what it might look like when you approach the edge, but before you leap. The first complication to consider is the matter of when you can expect your defined benefit payments and how the timing and amounts of those payments may or may not align with your plan to leap into retirement.

You will remember from the pension and social security section above, in the case of the social security program (and I will leave the parallel pension example for the reader who may benefit from a pension) there is a choice for one to make about when to begin receiving monthly income benefits. The example above involved the choice either to take $2,022 per month beginning at age 62, $2,890 at age 66 years plus eight months, or $3,672 at age 72. Which of those options is the best choice for the well-planned group that has built wealth and wants to retire before these defined benefits are available?

To answer that question we may ask "how much does each choice get me if I live to 90"? The clear winner there is to wait until age 72 and receive $925,000 total by age 90 instead of taking the age 62 option and only collecting $703,000. We might ask "if I wait and take the age 72 option, how many years do I have to live to bypass the age 62 option?" The math says that the age 72 option passes the age 62 option in total payout in your 79th year. Several of my friends and colleagues simply stop the thought process here and ask themselves, "do I really expect to live past 79 or should I take the age 62 option?"

I would suggest that we care less about the answer to that question and more about how a delay in starting defined monthly benefits affects our accumulated wealth, the 4% rule, and our management of risk over time. I would also suggest that if we deplete our accumulated wealth by more than our delayed monthly benefits make up for, then we may be in a financial death spiral. So do your arithmetic extremely carefully here. Financial death spirals can be hazardous to your financial health and are not to be included in your wealth plan.

If you stand at the edge of retirement at age 58 with $3.5 million in before-tax wealth (you figure $3.1 million after-tax) and a plan to spend $10,000 per month in retirement, then the 4% rule says you have done exceedingly well. Because your after-tax wealth fully pays for your lifestyle in retirement, you are free to delay these defined benefit payments until age 72 and hope to collect the full $925,000 by age 90. Maybe you can use that $925,000 to buy the Lexus you resisted the urge to splurge on earlier in life.

But if you stand at the edge of retirement at age 58 with only $2.7 million in before-tax investments (you figure $2.4 million after-tax) and hope to spend $10,000 each month, then you are short $2,000 per month. If you start down this path at age 58 you will deplete your wealth each year to pay for a lifestyle you cannot afford. When you reach age 62 and begin to collect $2,022 in social security, you will have decreased the value of your after-tax wealth to $2.3 million. This decreased after-tax wealth will only provide you with $7,600 per month. This added to your $2,022 from social security only provides $9,622 per month and you are spending $10,000. Death spiral. Do not try this at home...

You may examine the same scenario and ask, "what if I retire at 58 and wait to take the larger monthly payout at age 66 plus eight months or at age 72?" Your first look will be encouraging, but then I will remind you of our nasty enemy, inflation. If you truly account for inflation between your proposed retirement at age 58 and either of those two later payouts, you lose and wind up in deep trouble. Keep working your wealth plan. See you next October. Vote with this gap in your wealth plan in mind.

The concept here is that your wealth in-hand somehow represents a bridge to some other income or form of wealth at a time in the future. With defined benefit plans, like pensions and social security, you know how far into the future the bridge must extend. Knowing how far into the future your bridge must carry you makes it easier to differentiate between strong bridges and death spirals.

You should carefully consider the construction of your bridge if your wealth plan includes the notion of a future inheritance. An inheritance is, generally, some form of asset that will become yours at an unknown time in the future. Focus here on the words "unknown time" and remember our nasty enemy inflation.

You will remember that inflation is the rise of the average price of a basket of goods and services over time. If inflation in your wealth plan is budgeted at 2% each year, then your $10,000 per month spent in the first year of retirement will only buy you $8,330 worth of those same goods and services 10 years later.

Let's say that as you work your wealth plan while you are young, you expect to inherit $1 million from a parent who is 60 years old. You should begin to think about this far distant possibility by discounting the amount you expect to receive by the inflation rate for each year into the future. The actuarial tables that define the average expected life of an American say that someone who is 60 years old will live for 21.6 more years. If you take 2% off of the $1 million possible inheritance for 21.6 years, then you might be getting an inheritance that would be worth $667,000 now. That is precisely why you will plan for inflation in your wealth plan.

If you have been following along well to this point (and you might not if you are young or if you are not as young as you might like to be) you may notice that the $1 million inheritance through the 21.6 years has not been allowed (or assumed) to grow with the S&P 500 plus reinvested dividends. Good catch. But here is your truth as you consider the positive effect of any future inheritance: this is the future we are talking about and the future is unknown. Add to that the fact that the future of how a parent might invest or spend their money is out of your control. It is their free will (remember that one?) as to what they do with the wealth they have accumulated.

Within *your* free will, is how much cash you plan to accumulate before you leap, and you're going to want plenty of it. As you approach the edge, but before you leap, you will want to build your cash reserves to allow you to begin retirement without having to race to sell assets to buy groceries. This may seem like a stretch, but I want you to have two years of cash on hand before you leap. Two years. That's a lot of cash. If you are planning to spend $10,000 per month in retirement and your defined benefit payments don't begin for two years, then you will want $240,000 in cash on hand. If you are planning to spend $10,000 per month and your defined benefit payment is $3,000 per month on day one of your retirement, then you only need $168,000.

Why so much cash before you leap? Because if you leap with no cash and have to sell assets to buy groceries and the market starts to trend downward (remember markets go up and markets go down) you could be consuming more than your 4% early in your retirement and that is a problem. If you start early to shrink the pile of assets that are planned to fund your long retirement, you could be initiating your financial death spiral; we don't want to do that. A big stash of cash before you leap is a necessity.

When you approach the edge, but before you leap, you must ensure that your wealth plan is honest, complete, and does not contain any leaps of faith that result in a death spiral. This is an after-tax look at your investments in hand. It is a careful look at your spending in retirement, including those expense items that will continue to increase (like the property taxes on the home you own and the basket of goods and services you plan to consume) and some that will decrease (like health insurance as you enroll in Medicare). And it is a serious and conservative assessment of any bridges you are building to future sources of income or wealth. Best only to leap when you are fully prepared. Unleaping proves to be a difficult trick for most.

For those of you I am speaking to in this section, if you have followed my suggestions – chief among them that you work and adjust your after-tax cash needs in your planned retirement and the honest sources of these funds, that you retire your mortgage(s) if your 4% rule on your mortgage balance does not cover the monthly payment (and it will not), that you fully understand the real amounts and timing for any defined benefits (social security and pension) that you may have earned, that you heavily discount any future inheritance because it is beyond your control, and that you accumulate two years of cash before you leap – then I strongly urge you to read to the end. The section ahead is must-read material for you and you should become comfortable with the basics before you leap.

• • •

Living Well in Your Retirement

Congratulations, you have retired! Or as I still say – I am practicing being retired. My first thought for you is purely emotional but is important to share. If you are choosing to retire on your terms with a solid wealth plan, then you have done a good job at your chosen profession or line of work. And your chosen profession or line of work has done something for you for all these years that you need to recognize. Your chosen profession or line of work has stroked your ego for many years. Yes, your ego, and it's important for us to acknowledge that it's ok. Just know that when you choose to stop working, your chosen profession or line of work will stop stroking your ego. When that happens, you'll need to find other ways to feel good about yourself. Find a cause. Volunteer. Write a long story about wealth to your children. Just don't miss this one.

Now that you've reached this milestone, let's work through how to get at the money you'll need during your long retirement. I remember my Dad telling me a long time ago that I was to save money, I was to invest money, and I was never to spend my investments. I now understand that my Dad was really saying to never spend my investments, until I got to *this point* in life –retirement. This is when the wise harvesting of assets to produce after-tax spending money to pay for retirement becomes the priority. This is when we think through what we sell and why.

Let's start with the best scenario for those who worked a stellar wealth plan. If your defined benefit payments and the dividend payments from your SPY, IVV, and/or VOO holdings meet your monthly and annual after-tax spending needs, you might never need to sell an asset. Congrats. Enjoy. You can skip ahead to the next section. But if you need to take a little something out to supplement the defined benefits plus dividends then read on.

Conventional financial thinking (and watch out for that) says we should begin to spend our assets by drawing from our individual (or joint with rights of survivorship) investment account. But let's work on the word "conventional" before we actually sell any assets to buy groceries in our retirement. Conventional here is for an individual (or married couple) that has allowed their helper to manage their investment portfolio. When their helper manages this portfolio, he or she is actively buying and selling individual securities to justify their annual 1% fee. With their helper actively trading in this person's, or couple's, portfolio, it means they've been paying long and short-term capital gains taxes each year and the basis in their portfolio is close to market.

In our case, we purchased and held SPY, IVV, and/or VOO (and reinvested our dividends) for a long period of time. Because we held these positions, we have not yet paid long-term capital gains taxes and our basis is far below the market price. Conventional financial thinking tells that other individual (or married couple) to begin to liquidate their individual (or joint) investment account first because they have a small amount (if any) in capital gains and will therefore not owe taxes (because they already paid them). Remember, if that other individual (or married couple) took assets from their IRA (or 401(k)) account, these assets would be taxed as ordinary income. It all sounds harmless, until you realize that ordinary income taxes paid at 22% can take a big bite out of the dollars you need to buy groceries in retirement. That is why the conventional approach goes to the individual (or joint) investment account first in an effort to avoid taxes.

This conventional financial thinking does not work for us because we were not conventional investors. We grew our long-term capital gains in our individual (or joint with rights of survivorship) investment account, we grew ordinary income gains in our IRA and 401(k) accounts, and we grew never-to-be-taxed-again gains in our Roth IRA account. We need to carefully consider our options to find the best tax strategy before we start to sell assets. And because we accumulated a couple years of cash before we leaped off the edge into retirement, we have some time to figure this out.

The next round of financial thinking on getting at your retirement money would have you simultaneously pull assets from all of your investment accounts in hopes of minimizing taxes over your lifetime. This approach suggests that you take funds from your individual (or joint) investment account, your traditional IRA account, and your Roth IRA account in proportion to the assets in each. So if you had $1 million in each account, you would take equal before-tax amounts out of each account to meet your needs. This approach blends the 0% tax of Roth IRA withdrawals with the 15% long-term capital gains tax component of your individual (or joint) investment account withdrawals and the ordinary income tax component (remember, we planned at the 22% tax band in the work above) for the IRA withdrawals. Does this approach work for you? Only you can make that call; you'll need to do the work with the numbers that represent your situation. Only you know your income needs, your defined benefit payments, and how after-tax money can be withdrawn from your investment accounts in proportion to your before-tax balances.

There is one other approach to generating after-tax money to fund your retirement spending. This approach is likely unique to us because we bought SPY, IVV, and/or VOO, we reinvested our dividends, and we held these positions for a long time. This investing approach over long periods of time has produced large capital gains, and possibly some important capital gains taxes, as we sell some of these positions to buy groceries. Now we need to work through the possibility of paying no taxes on these long-term capital gains and not going to jail. Yes, no taxes and no jail. Sound too good to be true? Remember the section called "The Basics of Basis" and the "step up" basis on assets when someone dies? This approach allows you to "step up" your basis to market to avoid paying taxes and doesn't involve your passing away. It sounds like an option worthy of our time to explore, so let's.

The long-term capital gains tax rate in 2020 was 0% for a married couple filing a joint tax return if their taxable income was below $80,000. This rate jumps to 15% on taxable income above $80,000 and up to 20% on taxable income over $496,600. But before we go too far down this path, let's look at what the term "taxable income" might mean to us as we enter retirement and how a 0% bracket on long-term capital gains might help.

Taxable income (on your Form 1040 tax return) is the result of taking your gross income number and subtracting your deductions (either the standard deduction or your itemized deductions). Remember, Congress regularly changes the tax laws, so pay close attention and work on your annual wealth plan work in October before elections. The most recent tax reform legislation ushered in an increase in the standard deduction to $24,800 for married couples filing joint tax returns. That means that most of us now use the standard deduction instead of itemizing as we used to. For that reason, and for simplicity's sake, we'll use the current standard deduction to understand how the 0% long-term capital gains tax can help a long-term investor like us.

Let's start with the taxable income cap of $80,000 and add to that the standard deduction of $24,800. That means we can generate up to $104,800 in gross income and still pay no long-term capital gains taxes. Keep in mind that gross income is the sum of our wages, bank interest, dividends, IRA distributions, social security and pension benefits, and capital gains.

To illustrate how the 0% long-term capital gains tax might work for us, let's first work through the simplest example. Let's imagine we are newly retired at 60 years old, so our wages have gone to zero, and we are not yet old enough to apply for social security and are not yet receiving pension benefits. We followed the advice above and accumulated two years of cash before retiring so we don't need to generate cash to buy groceries right now, but as dictated by our wealth plan, we are planning for the future. In this situation, we likely have only taxable interest, dividends, and capital gains to make up our gross income. And in this example let's use the 0% long-term capital gains tax rate to "step up" our basis in our oldest shares of SPY, IVV, or VOO to market price and pay no taxes on our gains. Free money again, and your wealth plan likes free money.

If I expected to earn $40,000 in taxable interest and dividends on my holdings of SPY, IVV, and/or VOO (and on my cash holdings) during 2020, then I could also generate $64,800 in taxable long-term capital gains and pay no tax on the capital gains portion of my income. This is possible because the $40,000 in interest and dividends plus the $64,800 in long-term capital gains minus the standard deduction of $24,800 leaves us with only $80,000 of taxable income and – voila – we pay no taxes on our capital gains. It gets even better, this scenario puts us in the 12% tax bracket on interest and dividend income, instead of the 22 to 24% band we planned around – seems like a win all around.

Because we have a few years' worth of cash saved and because we want to take advantage of this 0% tax loophole on long-term capital gains, we are going to sell some of our oldest SPY, IVV, or VOO shares and then buy more of these shares at market price. We are only going to sell these shares from our individual (or joint with rights of survivorship) investment account because those are the shares where long-term capital gains taxes apply. But how many shares should we sell and how many should we then buy back at market price?

If my oldest shares of SPY are from 2009 (just after the mortgage-backed securities scandal so we were buying SPY at a two for one sale), my average purchase price was $100 per share. If I sell one share of SPY at the market price of $370, then my long-term capital gain is $270 for each share of SPY I sell. To determine how many shares we should sell and still qualify for the 0% tax bracket on long-term capital gains, we divide the $64,800 in tax-free long-term capital gains by the $270 gain per share and come up with 240 shares of SPY to sell.

The sale of these 240 shares of SPY will produce $88,800 in our individual (or joint) investment account. And, since we don't need cash right now, we will reinvest these funds back into SPY, IVV, or VOO and let them continue to grow. The point here is that we used the 0% long-term capital gains tax rate to move the basis of these shares from the price we paid in 2009 to the market price today *without having to pay any federal tax on these gains*. And there you have a means to "step up" your basis in your holdings to market without the unfortunate step of dying.

There is one more important rule for you to be aware of, though it will likely not impact you since we buy SPY, IVV, and VOO, reinvest our dividends, and hold these positions for a long time. The wash-sale rule tells us that we cannot sell shares at a loss and rebuy the same (or substantially similar) shares within 61 days and take the tax loss on the initial sale. However, since our sale of SPY shares was at a **gain** of $270 per share, we are completely free to buy new shares of SPY (or the substantially similar IVV or VOO) in just a couple of days when the cash from our sale settles in our investment account.

In the example above we were using our cash on hand to fund our retirement spending. Let's use the same figures and instead imagine we've depleted our accumulated cash and need money from the sale of SPY shares to help pay for groceries. In this scenario let's assume we have the same $40,000 of taxable interest and dividend income. We've also sold 240 shares of those 2009 SPY shares to generate $88,800 in cash and $64,800 in long-term capital gains that cost us zero dollars in taxes.

Let's say we need $10,000 per month in after-tax money to pay for the groceries in retirement. In this case we know that the $40,000 in taxable interest and dividends is actually $2,933 each month after paying 12% in taxes. The tax free $88,800 from the sale of the 2009 SPY shares is $7,400 each month and gets us to $10,330 with the interest and dividend money. So we managed to use the 0% tax rate on long-term capital gains, but how did we do with the 4% rule?

Suppose we have $1 million in each of our three accounts (individual/joint, IRA (or 401(k)), and Roth IRA), then the $88,800 before-tax sale of SPY shares and the planned $88,800 after-tax spending for groceries represents taking just over 3% of our holdings. In this example, we are living within the 4% rule. Congrats. But your arithmetic to create after-tax dollars to spend in retirement while taking advantage of the 0% long-term capital gains tax bracket (while it remains in existence) and living within the 4% rule may not always work out this well. You may have more work to do.

The method we used above to sell the oldest 240 shares of SPY is called the FIFO method. FIFO stands for first-in, first-out and calls for us to sell the oldest shares first and then move forward in time. The opposite is a method called LIFO (last-in, first-out) where we would sell the most recently acquired shares and then work back in time. These two methods will produce wildly different results when selling shares to use the 0% bracket to your advantage.

If in the above example we used the LIFO method, we would be selling shares of SPY purchased in 2020 for an average of $320 per share. That is a long-term capital gain of $50 on each share and means we could sell 1,296 shares to consume our $64,800 long-term capital gain with no tax. This sale of 1,296 shares to maximize our tax savings would provide over $479,000 in proceeds, which I think is way more cash than we need to buy groceries and is in flagrant violation of the 4% rule.

I would suggest that a tool you want to think through is called the specific-shares method. This is what Investopedia tells us about the specific-shares method: "The specific-shares method only works if certain conditions are met. The method requires that the investor has purchased multiple lots of the same security at different prices, is selling only some of the investor's shares in a stock and has kept a record of the cost basis of each stock or fund purchase." The word "lot" here is just the financial word for a set of shares you bought at the same time and at the same price.

You will fit this definition perfectly and here is why. You purchased multiple lots because you bought a new lot each month when you invested your savings and reinvested your dividends. And because you did this over a long period of time, the prices of each lot were different. As in the above definition, you are only selling some of your holdings – just enough to get $64,800 (in our example) in long-term capital gains so you can buy groceries. And you counted on Fidelity, Vanguard, and/or Schwab to keep track of your cost basis for each purchase of SPY, IVV, and/or VOO. Perfect. So now which lot(s) of shares should you sell to get the $64,800?

As we consider the answer to that question, I would urge you, at this time of your life – in retirement, to remain aware of the changing tax laws. I would encourage you to stay knowledgeable of the cost basis of your investments in SPY, IVV, and VOO in your investment accounts and the current tax consequences of each; be mindful of how you will maximize the after-tax monies of your defined benefit programs, and of course, continue to respect the 4% rule.

When you work on the before-tax and after-tax meaning of money invested in your individual (or joint with rights of survivorship) investment account, you will understand the usefulness of the specific-lot method not only to select shares to sell in order to minimize long-term capital gains taxes, but to maximize cash for your retirement and to live within the 4% rule.

When you look at your IRA (or 401(k)) and Roth IRA accounts for cash to fund your retirement spending, you will find that the cost basis, and therefore the specific-lot method no longer matters. As we previously established, the cost basis of your IRA holdings are essentially equal to zero (this money was never taxed on the way in) and your withdrawals are taxed as ordinary income.

In the example above, we sold 240 shares of 2009 SPY from our individual (or joint) investment account to generate $64,800 in long-term capital gains and got to spend the entire $88,800 on groceries because we owed no taxes on that sale. However, if we sell 240 shares of 2009 SPY from our IRA (or 401(k)) account and withdraw this to fund our retirement, then we cannot count on spending that same $88,800 on groceries because we first have to pay the tax man. And we have to pay the tax man a lot because this $88,800 distribution from our IRA is taxed as ordinary income and we planned our tax rate at 22-24%. That means that $20,000 goes to the tax man and we only have $68,800 left to spend in retirement. Do your homework and live in the after-tax dollars you can spend in your retirement.

Now let's look at your Roth IRA and see what happens when we sell 240 shares of 2009 SPY from that account. You will remember that you probably needed $2,440 (if you were earning $50,000 at the time) to put $2,000 into your Roth IRA because Roth IRA deposits are made after paying taxes on your ordinary income. The good news is that because you paid the tax man in the beginning, you don't have to pay taxes again in retirement when you take distributions from your Roth IRA account. So when we sell 240 shares of 2009 SPY, all $88,800 in proceeds are good for groceries in retirement, no Federal taxes to worry about!

In order to live well in your retirement, you must plan for saving and investing when you are young. You must look carefully at consumption and saving each year when you sit down with your wealth plan (maybe in October because it is before the year-end holidays and before the election) and you must make commitments to monthly investing and to what you will do with your next raise. To live well in your retirement, you and your wealth plan will follow a long and disciplined path as you move through life together. Two stages we've discussed, being young and not being as young as you might like, will give your wealth plan space to grow with our old friend, time. And you know this by now, but remember to invest each month, reinvest your dividend, and hold your positions in SPY, IVV, and/or VOO for a long time.

• • •

Share the Workload – And the Knowledge

Most couples develop patterns or ingrained behaviors through many years of marriage or partnership and raising a family together. Someone cooks, someone mows the lawn, someone buys the groceries, and someone pays the bills. If you do this wrong over many years, then one person knows the investment plan for retirement and the other person is in the dark. One person knows what is in each investment account and the other person doesn't even know the password to log into the Fidelity or Vanguard accounts. This lack of shared knowledge has come to trouble me greatly.

I make no judgements on how you manage your wealth plan, but I will offer you this: if you are fortunate enough to retire with someone you love, find the time to share the knowledge about how your wealth plan works and the role your loved one will play if you pass first. If your wealth plan involves providing for two people for a long and happy retirement, I feel you have a responsibility to empower your other half to share the workload, to share the knowledge, and for your other half to share a confident ability to carry on if you should pass first.

So, please, open a nice bottle of wine on a beautiful afternoon, in a place you both love, and share the workload and the knowledge.

• • •

Epilogue

I began writing this story with the sole intent to fulfill my Dad's wish that my daughters learn to grow and manage wealth through their lifetimes. It took me 10 years, after my Dad's passing, to realize how simple his wish had been, that it was there in front of me all along, but I had not yet engaged in a process to address his important request. It was the weekend of the Masters Tournament in April 2019 when I took pen to paper. Tiger Woods won the Masters on that Sunday afternoon, April 14, in Augusta, Georgia. By the end of the weekend Tiger was wearing his fifth green jacket and I had an outline for a story to share with my daughters about wealth and wealth management over long periods of time. It was a weekend I will never forget.

Our daughters both read an early version of this story before visiting us in Florida in February 2020. We discussed the story both together as a family and one-on-one, as we walked the beach and watched the sunsets from the balcony. Our daughters deeply appreciated the story and recognized how it provided a roadmap for developing and managing wealth over their lifetimes. I was surprised when they each told me how important this story would be for their friends who did not yet have anyone whispering this message of a wealth plan in their ears. They told me of friends in deep credit card debt without a greater appreciation for the road ahead. They told me that they wished this story of creating and managing wealth was required curriculum back in their high school days.

This perspective of my daughters paralleled other discussions I have had over time with friends and colleagues about their financial road ahead. While these discussions may have been short and superficial at times, I became aware that maybe we had a level of knowledge, or perspective, to share. Most people I spoke with either did not have a wealth plan or did not know how to convey these important thoughts to their family and loved ones.

After our girls flew home from Florida, I began to edit our family version of the story to create a copy that could be shared with others. My goal was to craft a readable and informative story that can be read and reread over time, by people beyond the family circle of grandchildren that my Dad addressed in his final wishes to us.

I spent portions of the next three weeks revising my draft before we cut our Florida trip short and flew home on news of the emergence of the worldwide coronavirus pandemic. Without real intent, I put the story away until we returned to our beloved lake in Maine for the summer. At that time, I was thrilled to engage our oldest daughter as my editor for this story and we exchanged drafts throughout the season. Again, without intent, this story was placed on a back burner when we returned home in the fall and only came back to front-and-center in January 2021.

These two periods of hiatus were about four months each. That was not ever the plan, it just happened. Not being an experienced writer, I would imagine that these periods of walking away from your work may be common and helpful in reestablishing some important perspective. This period from March 2020 until now has been dominated by the coronavirus and its impact on people, nations, and economies around the world.

I do not feel qualified or capable of commenting on the medical, ethical, social, or political issues related to the response to the worldwide pandemic, or on the development and rollout of the various vaccines now being delivered. However, I do feel that the message of our wealth plan, delivered in the preceding pages, should be fairly tested against this once-in-a-century crisis, as this crisis has played out in economies and equity markets around the globe.

When I picked the story back up at the lake last summer, I began this epilogue feeling that some reflection and commentary on the financial impact of the COVID-19 pandemic, and the impact on your wealth plan, could not be overlooked. I now feel that leaving those words of summer 2020 as originally written fits our honest look back. This sentiment is preserved in these quotes from my original efforts at an epilogue:

"The four-month period in which I did not read or edit this story includes the emergence and spread of the worldwide coronavirus pandemic. As of this writing, COVID-19 has killed more than 180,000 Americans and dramatically, if temporarily, upset financial markets."

"The SPY index fund reached a record high above $339 on February 19 and fell to $223 on March 23, a 34% drop in value in just 33 calendar days. The world had never experienced a financial loss of this magnitude in this short a time ever. In the weeks that followed, the nation's unemployment figures went from close to zero to more than 20% of all American workers. That is one in five Americans out of work."

"It has been a terrifying time, but even in the midst of this financial hemorrhage, we held true to the story told here. We sold none of our holdings. We did not panic. We did not run for the exits. Instead, we executed on the advice above that when the markets go down it is a great time to buy at discounted prices. We (our daughters included) began to buy shares on Monday, April 6 when SPY traded at $261 per share. On August 19 – just six months after the February 19 SPY high – the SPY fund returned to $339 per share. That represents a 30% return on our investment in SPY shares at $261 in just six months."

As I work to finish this story on Super Bowl weekend 2021 with the Chiefs and the Buccaneers set to play on Sunday night in Tampa Bay, the reported cases of COVID-19 in the United States have surpassed 26.7 million and reported deaths have climbed to more than 456,000. The coronavirus pandemic is reported to have killed more than 2.7 million worldwide. Our country has struggled through a difficult year with fiery debate over the real nature of the pandemic and the steps to combat it, over racial injustice with protestors killed in our streets, and a contested presidential election that has ushered in a Democratic president and Democratic Congress for the first time since the 111th Congress in 2009-2011.

Again, I will not comment on the medical, ethical, social, or political challenges of our current times. I will, however, reflect on this troubling year through the lens of our wealth plan and the reactions of the markets.

As noted above, the SPY index fund reached an all-time high on February 19, 2020 at $339 per share and plummeted 34% to $223 in just 33 calendar days, 23 trading days. The SPY index fund, and the markets in general, returned to historic highs just six months later as financial markets looked past what was perceived to be the temporary nature of the pandemic and to expected levels of corporate earnings after widespread distribution of effective vaccines. At the close on the Friday afternoon before the 2021 Super Bowl, the SPY index fund was at $387, a 14% gain on the February high and a 73% gain over the March lows.

Having started this story on Masters Weekend in April 2019 when Tiger Woods won his fifth green jacket, I found it fitting that I finished this work on Super Bowl weekend in February 2021 when Tom Brady won his seventh Lombardi trophy. The championship runs of these two men have spanned two decades. And they were both 43 years old at the time of their latest victories. I hope you too find success with your chosen profession, your personal wealth plan, and that your run with your wealth plan will span a long period of time. I hope you will begin this process early in life, or as early as possible, and find the process to be of value over your lifetime.

The fundamental message of our wealth plan is to take the long run to building wealth, to understand that the market goes up and goes down, and to make consistent and predetermined investments on a regular basis regardless of the ups and downs in the short run. If you followed this advice, you would have bought SPY, IVV, and/or VOO in March when your friends were running for the exits. If you followed this advice, you would have been buying shares at a one third off sale and lowering your average price per share. And you would have been handsomely rewarded as markets returned to push new record heights.

I hope you will take from this a confident view of the long run – maybe the 50-year long run. I hope you will sit deliberately once a year and work your wealth plan to a financial destination of your choosing and on your own schedule. I hope your wealth plan will develop and mature as you move through the stages of your life. I hope you will find that sharing this knowledge with your loved ones – spouse, significant other, or your children and grandchildren – is a helpful, necessary, and fulfilling step in the dialogue about wealth, the management of wealth, and the behavior leading to wealth.

I have greatly enjoyed this long and varied process to express a body of information, thought, and reason that I deeply believe fulfills my Dad's request. I hope you will find the perspective shared here to be helpful in creating and managing your own wealth plan to a destination of your choosing.

You will remember early on I made a simple request. I asked that when you were done with this story – either for the first time, the second time, or after you might share it with someone you love – that you please provide feedback to help me better guide the next readers to a wealth plan of their chosen destination. Please drop me an email with your thoughts at thepersonalwealthplan@gmail.com. I thank you for any and all thoughts you might be willing to share.

I hope you are able to enjoy this as much as I have. Thank you for reading. Be safe, be well, and good luck.

David S. Upton

• • •

Made in the USA
Middletown, DE
22 October 2021

50833529R00066